W9-BJM-767

E. Fedorov

MAN and NATURE

THE ECOLOGICAL CRISIS
AND SOCIAL PROGRESS

INTERNATIONAL PUBLISHERS,
New York

Library of Congress Cataloging in Publishing Data

Fedorov Evgeni Konstantinovich, 1910-
MAN AND NATURE.

Based on the author's Vzaimodeistvie obshchestva i
prirody, 1972.

1. Human ecology. 2. Social policy. I. Fedorov,
Evgeni Konstantinovich, 1910-. Vzaimodeistivie obshchetva
i prirody. II. .Title.

Robert Manning Strozier Library

JUL 12 1982

Tallahassee, Florida

GF41.F42   304.2   80-202
ISBN 0-7178-0573-5
ISBN 0-7178-0567-0 pbk.

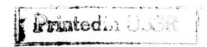
Printed in U.S.R

CONTENTS

ERRATA

Page 162, line 6 from the bottom

Should read:
United Nations and its specialised agencies, must be vested with

Зак. 2300.

PREFACE BY THE AUTHOR

I am happy to be able to offer the reader a book devoted to what I consider one of the most important global problems of civilization today.

This book is based largely on my earlier works, *The Interaction of Society and Nature* and *The Ecological Crisis and the Social Progress,* published in the USSR in 1972 and 1977 respectively. (17)

Since then a great many new studies on this subject have appeared, and some of the relevant problems have been debated at a number of national and international conferences in which I took part.

My most sincere thanks go to my colleagues—scientists and public figures—in other countries who took part in the Dartmouth Conference and the Pugwash Conference and other international meetings, and to my colleagues at the World Meteorological Organization. Many a time did we argue over points in this book, and over our often diiffering views on the subject. But it is these very discussions that gave me new ideas, made me seek new arguments and then alter and define more precisely some of my earlier theses.

Despite differences of opinion, all of us must be clear about one thing—humanity must adopt new methods in order to optimize its relationships with nature. And no matter what course is taken, this can be done only in conditions of a lasting peace, disarmament, peaceful coexistence and close cooperation between countries with different social systems. There are no alternatives, and I hope this book will advance the understanding and recognition of that basic truth.

INTRODUCTION

Interaction between man and nature is inseparable from the very history of humanity. It is the highest form of interaction between life in general and the environment.

It is now common knowledge that organic life, which began about three billion years ago, played a tremendous role in the creation of the atmosphere, the hydrosphere and the veneer of the earth's crust, all of which make up the planet we know today. For example, oxygen in the atmosphere is the result of the vital activity of plants. Limestone in its different forms, whether in large deposits on land or in coral reefs and atolls in the ocean, has been created by minute marine animals. And the soil is the product of the combined action of all living things and natural processes which are taking place on the surface of our planet, on the boundary between the atmosphere and the lithosphere. The same applies to the interaction of the land and the sea.

The celebrated Soviet scientist Academician Vladimir Vernadsky wrote:

> The exchange of matter between land and sea is set in motion by two main physico-geographical processes. Most of the chemical elements that enter the hydrosphere come from the lithosphere where they are carried by rivers, and the bulk of matter returns from the hydrosphere into the lithosphere by way of a complicated precipitation of substances from aquatic solutions. . . . The composition and character of the substances carried in solution form, by rivers, are largely determined by various life phenomena. The same applies to the chemical processes which actuate the precipitation of chemical elements in the form of solid compounds from seawater. (12)

Seawater is to all intents and purposes a weak salt solution; it is far from the saturation point, and consequently precipitation of solids from it can occur only biochemically, that is, through the vital activity of living organisms.

The diversity of life forms evolved over hundreds of millions of years, and their adaptation to different, often extreme, environmental conditions are amazing. We find living things on mountaintops and in conditions of eternal cold, in places where air pressure is only about one-fifth that at sea level, or in the hot, near-boiling water of geysers, in the eternal darkness, dampness and cold of deep subterranean caves, and in oceanic troughs under conditions of tremendous pressure.

At the same time, each individual animal or plant species can exist within a comparatively narrow range of ambient conditions, using the resources of the environment and exerting an influence on it in a definite and invariable way, predetermined by its biological mechanism. New forms of interaction with the environment emerged only at a time when new plant and animal species came into being through the slow process of biological evolution. That was long before the advent of human beings.

Later, the situation changed fundamentally. Remaining almost completely unchanged himself, biologically speaking, man has continually and at an increasing rate been changing the forms and modes of his interaction with the environment.

At one time this interaction was between a weak, helpless being and a vast incomprehensible world of the elements. Nature and its resources were inexhaustible, practically infinite compared to the needs of the small human population of our planet. The power of the elements that bore down on man appeared truly infinite compared to his meager capabilities. Originally, the all but insuperable difficulties of the natural environment gave him little leeway in his activities. But with time—slowly at first, and then more rapidly—the situation began to change.

The persistent work which stimulated the development of intelligence, and the felicitous ability to combine the meager strength of one individual into a pool of strength of a collective enabled human beings to score initial successes in protecting themselves from the elements and later fighting them.

The interaction of human beings with nature began at the time they separated themselves from the natural environment. And that became possible through the creation of primary, primitive forms of social organization. Since then, the natural processes and factors that depend on the structure and other characteristics of our planet, and the social processes and factors that depend on the structure and characteristics of society have been closely interwoven.

Speaking of nature, we mean actually the section of the universe that is known to us today. However, in practical terms, relations between man and nature take shape within his habitat.

Over hundreds of millennia, communities of people lived in fairly small areas. It was only several thousands of years ago that tribes began to develop contacts, barter goods and launch military campaigns to distant lands, although at that time these were limited to one continent. The first more or less correct notions of what our planet was like, of its oceans and continents and of the peoples who lived on it were formed a mere 300 or 400 years ago.

Until then the earth's surface was a vast area with isolated or loosely associated foci of human activity. The isolated and basically self-sufficient existence and development of such communities—indeed, whole civilizations—in different regions of our planet terminated by the onset of the nineteenth century. In the epoch of colonial conquests, there began the process of emergence of a world economy and extensive international relations.

Today the movement of people and the traffic of commodities pose no problems. Worldwide economic contacts have such great influence on the economy of most countries that only a very few, the largest of them, would be able to maintain their economies at the present level if they shut themselves up within their territorial boundaries. Global contacts are developing in the area of economics, politics, science and culture. The world is, in fact, becoming more and more integrated, and it is not surprising that it is in our time that man has broken through into outer space.

A mere twenty years ago the launching of the Earth's first man-made satellite ushered in the space age. Since then, automatic space probes have brought information about the Moon's surface and samples of its soil, have reached the planets Mars and Venus, and are transmitting back to Earth singular data about outer space over hundreds of millions of miles. People have learned how to live and work in near space and on the Moon, and are preparing for the day when interplanetary travel will be possible. Scientists have developed a fairly clear idea, albeit based on very indirect information, about the structure of the universe to a distance of about 10^{22} kilometers.

The population of the earth is growing rapidly, and by the year 2 000 it might well exceed the 6-billion mark. The utilization of natural resources will grow accordingly.

There are two kinds of resources: nonrenewable (mineral wealth), of which there is a certain fixed amount in the world; and renewable resources (fresh water in rivers, oxygen in the atmosphere, the forests and the biological mass), which come from the natural processes taking place on earth and are balanced between annual increase and annual consumption, including the utilization by human beings.

The term "natural resource" has not only a purely scientific or technological meaning but a historical one, too. At one time many elements of the natural environment meant nothing to humans. A mere 50 years ago uranium was regarded as nothing but a by-product in the extraction of radium. At present almost all resources—both renewable and nonrenewable—are used in the national economy, and their utilization has been intensified, especially over the past two-three decades. Today that part of many nonrenewable resources that has already been used up is fairly large in relation to their total known resources on our planet.

Also drawn into man's economic activities on an ever increasing scale are renewable resources. In many countries some of the renewable resources, such as soil, forest, water power and fresh water are used in their entirety.

Let us see how the environment influences man and what reciprocal influence society exerts on nature.

Primitive people could exist only within a very narrow range of natural conditions, whereas today there is hardly a place on the earth's surface, in the ocean and even in near space where human beings would not be able to live and work. The various types of human activity are becoming more and more independent of environmental conditions. A modern ship can cross the ocean in any wind or storm. Air transport can also operate in practically any weather conditions.

The transmission of gas, oil and electric power over long distances has obviated the necessity of building industries next to the sources of energy, as was previously the case.

The construction industry has over the past 40-50 years lost its seasonal character. We could cite many more instances of our growing independence from the natural environment.

All this does not mean, however, that environmental factors and conditions no longer have an effect on our activities. Quite the contrary, the more independent of the environment our actions become, the more fully must we take into account its properties and conditions in order to be able to do our work in the most expedient and effective manner.

Technical progress has made it imperative to take into account more and more features of the natural environment. Thus, in order to ensure stable radio transmission over long distances we have had to obtain information about the structure of the ionosphere. To make submarine navigation possible requires knowledge about the structure of the ocean deeps. In other words, we require the kind of information about the natural environment that in earlier days might have been of general interest to a small number of scientists.

With the growth of the population and the development of production, man himself began to influence the environment more and more. These changes in the environment, just like the changes that emerge as a result of the vital activity of any other association of living beings, consist of the transformation of the structure of the environment, its energy balance, its composition, and the cyclic movement of the substances of which it is made. But the interaction of animals and plants with the environment produces slow biological evolution, whereas the effect of human activity on the environment grows very rapidly, both overall and per capita. The antropogenic effect on nature is growing because humans modify, that is, develop, all forms of their interaction with the environment, and transform, in the words of Academician Vernadsky, "the technology of life" itself.

All these forms of interaction are closely tied in with each other. For example, while extracting mineral wealth, burning fuel, or irrigating crops on arid land, we extract certain substances from the natural environment. While discharging industrial and agricultural waste and other such byproducts into the atmosphere and hydrosphere, we introduce new components into the environment. By improving marshlands or piping water for household and industrial needs, we alter some of the elements of moisture circulation: the fluvial runoff into the ocean is reduced and the intensity of evaporation on the continents increases. Transformations taking place on the earth's surface inevitably affect the energy balance of the earth-atmosphere system. One way this balance is affected is through changes in the albedo (reflective power) of the earth's surface.

The energy balance of our planet is also affected by changes in the transparency of the atmosphere and by the discharge of heat into the atmosphere as a result of man's production activities.

Now, how much do we actually affect the elemental processes taking place on our planet?

Changes in the structure of the earth's surface—plowing up plains and cutting down trees to clear areas for agricultural uses, building cities, roads and water reservoirs, etc.—have taken up about 20 percent of the land.

This "cultured" surface has thus become "smoother", not so "rough", and the area of evaporation has increased, affecting the turbulence of the air in the lower atmospheric layers and causing shifts in the energy balance.

Large cities—giant heat generators—stimulate the convection of the air above them and so increase atmospheric precipitation.

The masses of water drawn from rivers for the needs of irrigation and industry form about 20 percent of the world's runoff, but in many areas (over a large part of the United States, in almost the whole of Western Europe, and in the south of the European part of the Soviet Union) it exceeds 100 percent; that is, the entire runoff is put through industrial enterprises, water mains, sewers, and irrigation systems.

The total rock mass extracted from the earth's crust is infinitesimally small compared with the mass of the planet as a whole, but for some of the substances the amount extracted constitutes a sizable proportion of their total reserves and has substantially altered the natural course of their circulation about our planet.

Industrial and other wastes discharged into the atmosphere and hydrosphere contain substances which in the past did not exist in a natural state, such as many synthetic products.

Over the past 50 years, radiation from our planet in the radio-frequency range has increased hundreds of times. If there are civilizations somewhere in the universe capable of registering and measuring radiation from celestial bodies in this range of the electromagnetic spectrum, the way we do it here on earth, they could have registered some changes in its intensity.

A clue to the changes in the energy balance is provided by the amount of energy obtained or converted by human beings in the process of their activities. A primitive tribal community of about 100 members could in the course of work develop power amounting to several kilowatts, whereas today we wield power totaling about 10^9 kilowatts (kw) in the form of energy sources of long duration (power stations, different mechanisms, etc.).

Compared with the energy radiated by the Sun (10^{23} kw), or the energy of the movement and rotation of the Earth, 10^9 kw is an infinitesimal amount. Nevertheless, it is comparable with the energy of the processes taking place on the surface of our planet, in the atmosphere and in the ocean. These processes, which determine the diversity of climate and weather on earth, are set in motion by the stream of solar energy that falls on the sunward part of the planet. The power of this stream is on the order of 10^{13} kw.

The energy resources used by man amount to only a tiny fraction of this figure. We must not, however, regard this correlation as a limit to our ability to influence the elements. In actual fact, as we shall see later, this ability is much greater.

The point is that the natural environment is not a stable structure. The continual elemental processes taking place in the atmosphere and in the ocean—movements of masses of air and water, moisture circulation and other phenomena—are closely interconnected.

The interconnection of natural phenomena and their sporadic instability make the environment highly sensitive. Therefore, even with limited technological means, man may interfere with delicately poised natural processes.

Modification of natural phenomena is sometimes induced by an unpremeditated side effect of man's activity and often against his will.

To sum up our description of the interaction between society and nature, we can note that today people

⊙ are familiar with the entire surface of the globe and almost all of it has become the scene of their practical work;

⊙ have begun the exploration of outer space;

⊙ have expanded the physical limits of their existence by learning to protect themselves from inclement conditions in any place on the surface of the earth, in near space and in the ocean;

⊙ have drawn into their activities almost all the elements of the natural environment, both renewable and nonrenewable, some of them to a considerable extent or almost in full, and others so far in a very small degree;

⊙ need more and more information about the state of the natural environment;

⊙ have intensified their activities in a way that noticeably (and often harmfully to themselves) alters the established patterns of cyclic movement of matter, affecting the natural course of elemental phenomena on the surface of the earth. Man is beginning to master the methods of control over some of them and is trying to utilize them for military purposes.

All this taken together means that we have entered a new phase in our relationships with the environment—that of fully utilizing the possibilities of our home planet.

Remarkably, having acquired the capability to transform nature, having emerged into outer space, having largely thrown off the constraints on our activities originally imposed by natural conditions, we have encountered other constraints and can no longer regard terrestrial resources as inexhaustible or unlimited. More and more often we have to reckon with the limits and size of everything that exists on earth.

What will happen next?

Many economists, sociologists and naturalists are studying the processes of interaction between man and nature in the light of the facts they have at their disposal and the data they have extrapolated for the future.

The rapidly growing power-to-people ratio and our growing ability to change the face of the earth, give enough reason for optimistic prognostications about the future of the humankind.

> With the emergence of a rational being, our planet has entered a new stage of its history: the biosphere has changed into the noosphere.* Moreover, we seem to be breaking through the confines of the earth, since everything points to the fact that the geochemical action of the intelligence of civilized man cannot be limited to the size of our planet, wrote Academician Vernadsky in 1944. (13)

Tsiolkovsky, Shklovsky, Clarke, and many other Soviet and foreign scientists referred to the future of human society as a continuous advance utilizing our own planet, the solar system and the distant worlds of the universe.

At the same time, over the past two centuries, and especially during the past several decades, another line and, accordingly, another concept of the "man and nature" problem has taken shape.

The depletion of resources, the growing impact of man on nature, and above all the pollution of the environment, and the possibility that it may be modified for hostile purposes, are matters of growing concern in many countries.

This concern is heightened by the crises which have rocked the capitalist world: the energy crisis; growing food shortages, which are alleged to have been caused by a growing population in the developing countries; the disruption of the monetary system, etc.

The interaction of people and the environment is closely linked with the problems of development in countries which lag behind others economically, technically and culturally. The widening gap between living standards in the advanced and the backward countries is causing anxiety in scientific and political circles, as well as the public at large.

The determination of the developing countries to raise the

---

* The biosphere as altered consciously or unconsciously.—*Ed.*

levels of their development, to speed up their economic growth, largely depends on rational utilization of their abundant natural resources and on the character of their economic relations with other nations.

All these problems are discussed at international conferences and at UN-sponsored symposiums and seminars.

At two of its special sessions the UN General Assembly discussed the problem of a new international economic order that would establish a more equitably pattern of worldwide economic exchange and would boost the development of the economically and technically backward countries.

The United Nations Trade and Development Board and a host of other international organizations and conferences have discussed ways and means of making the most effective and rational use of the wealth of the world ocean. Also active is the International Union for the Conservation of Natural Resources.

The results of all these activities have so far been rather limited. Nevertheless, agreements have already been reached on reducing pollution from waste dumped from ships into the world ocean. Also, principles have been worked out to exercise systematic observation and control, under an integrated program and via a worldwide monitoring system, over the state of the natural environment and the changes in it wrought by humans. The majority of countries have ratified the international convention on the prohibition of military or any other hostile use of environment modification techniques.

By contrast, the question of a new economic order is still in the discussion stage.

More resolute and promising proposals have been put forward by individual authors and various international scientific and public organizations (the Pugwash movement, the Dartmouth conferences, the International Federation of Institutes of Advanced Study, the International Institute for Peace in Vienna) which are not committed to any particular government for their decisions.

In 1970 a group of political figures, businessmen and scientists set up the so-called Club of Rome, a small international organization whose members, acting in a "private capacity", have concerned themselves with mankind's future development.

Environmental protection and the rational use of natural resources, and a host of other problems, including those facing the
newly developing countries, have been discussed at conferences
of various international public organizations, such as the World
Congress of Peace Forces, nongovernmental organizations for disarmament and many others. The results of this research and the
views discussed have been published in books and in the press.

The old Malthusian thesis of the overpopulation of the earth
also comes up occasionally in these publications.

The earth cannot support the existing population, let alone the
population that we expect to have several decades from now. The
demographic explosion—the bomb of overpopulation—is the main
danger which will eventually, possibly soon, bring humankind to
the verge of catastrophe. This is a rather widespread view which
has many followers in the West. Its authors hold that the developing countries should curb population growth, because otherwise they will not be able to feed themselves.

Significantly, the earlier extrapolation of how much our rapidly growing population will consume and how long the resources
of the earth will last has given way to comprehensive overall analysis of the activities of human society.

The first attempt of this kind was made by Jay W. Forrester,
the author of *World Dynamics* (1971) (30). Another book which
follows much the same line of argument is *The Limits to Growth,*
written by D. H. Meadows et al. (USA, 1972) (41). There were
some other books on the subject commissioned by the Club of
Rome. In these and other studies the principal economic indicators—such as industrial and agricultural growth, the rate of birth
and death, environmental pollution, etc. averaged out for mankind
as a whole, fit into one integral system of mathematical proportions.

By evaluating, with a large measure of subjectivity, and on the
basis of data collected over the past several decades, the characteristics of the direct connections and feedbacks between these
indicators, the authors try to predict a course of events for the
future. The result is very depressing indeed. If the present trends
and character of social development are retained, then, they say,
in about 50-70 years, the population of our planet, which will
then be about 6.5 billion, will begin to die out because of a short-

age of natural resources and from the insupportable pollution of the environment. Only after more than two-thirds of the world's population has perished will it be possible for the remaining one-third to subsist with any degree of hope for the future.

What if the growth of population is held up? It is true, they say, that this would delay the catastrophe, but it would not fundamentally change the course of events. The problem is not just population growth as such but growth in general, that immanent desire for expansion and augmentation which is intrinsic to any social system, and in any society. Therefore, according to these authors, it is necessary to arrest all development and growth—in industry, consumption and population. It is only a state of global balance that can save mankind from catastrophe.

Research was carried on by M. Mesarovic (USA) and E. Pestel (FRG) with funds provided by the Club of Rome. The product of this research is their book *Mankind at the Turning Point* (USA, 1974) (42). The authors discussed forty-one countries, or rather groups of countries: advanced capitalist countries, the socialist countries of Europe (together with the Soviet Union), developing countries and other groups of countries. But the authors skirted the analysis of the social distinctions (of paramount importance in this case) that make these countries so different. What they did, though, was to present these countries as specified geographical regions of the world, dividing them roughly into the "rich" and the "poor" nations. Using the systems analysis, it has since been proved that the global development of humanity is not only inevitable but that it is necessary. However, it must be "organic", i.e., akin to the growth of a living organism, each part of which develops in strict conformity with the growth of the organism as a whole.

The researchers demand that a well-coordinated policy be carried out in order to determine the rates and character of the economic development of countries, and the interaction between them. An accelerated rate of economic growth in the developing "poor" countries can be attained in large measure by lowering the overall rate of economic development in all countries and, in particular, by bringing down the rate of consumption in the advanced "rich" countries.

By emphasizing the close economic relationship between all

countries of the world, the authors are trying to convince their readers that this "organic" integrated development not only is the sole option left but also happens to be the most suitable for the "rich" countries in terms of the long-term interests of their population, and not merely for the immediate selfish interests of certain powerful monopoly groups.

Similar ideas have been set forth in many other recent publications, such as *Human Requirements, Supply Levels and Outer Bounds* (40) by John McHale and Magda Cordell McHale; a draft of the *State of the Planet Statement,* prepared by the Chairman of the Council of Trustees of the International Federation of Institutes for Advanced Study, Dr. Alexander King (37); the paper "What Now?" drafted by a group of researchers at the request of the Dag Hammarskjöld Foundation (50); the materials of the conference of Global Problems of Modern Civilisation sponsored by the International Institute for Peace in Vienna (32, 46); the study carried out by a group of scientists under Professor Jan Tinbergen on the development of a new world order; the paper entitled "Food for a Doubling World Population" (39) prepared by Hans Linnemann; and books and articles by Richard Folk (29), Barry Commoner (26), Edward Teller (49), and some others.

We have listed only those books which have a direct bearing on the problem of interaction between man and nature, and have left out many studies on purely economic problems in the developing countries.

In addition to the general and quite obvious basic thesis about the impossibility of the unlimited growth of population, production and consumption on our planet with its limited resources, space and mass, these studies also offer various concepts of the general crisis as it relates to these factors, and a variety of views on the ways and means of forestalling it.

We can also point out that during the past several years many authors have devoted more attention to the role played by social factors in the interaction of man and nature. However, in their examination of the social phenomena leading to a world crisis most of these scholars, without good reason, project the social factors characteristic of one particular social system on to other forms of social organization and, moreover, refer to them as a kind of immanent laws governing the development of human society.

These scholars also ignore the fact that changes in the social structure of society are inevitable, and this must certainly be taken into account in evaluating the present situation and in attempting to forecast and plan the ecological future of humankind.

Despite all the differences in their views, the authors agree on certain provisions, the most important of which, in our opinion, are the following:

⊙ if the present character and the rate of growth and development of humankind are to continue, they will inevitably lead to the emergence, in about 50-100 years, of a very serious ecological crisis, which will be tantamount to a collapse of modern civilization; and

⊙ it will be possible to avoid the crisis, if an overall long-term plan of action for the whole of humanity is drawn up in time (or *now*, considering the exponential character of society's development and its "inertia") and measures are taken on a global scale to prevent eruption of the crisis.

As for the differences in the authors' views, these concern mostly specific features of the structure, activities and development of modern society that exert a hazardous impact on the natural environment, and the ways and means of preventing the crisis. Some authors are of the opinion that any kind of development must be stopped altogether, and that the clock must even be turned back for human civilization. Others believe that the development of mankind is possible if certain conditions are observed.

In substance, the problem should be formulated this way: until when, how, and under what conditions can human beings develop within the limited space of our planet? Below we shall set forth our views on this problem.

In discussing the existence and development of humankind on our spatially limited planet, we must first of all estimate the possibilities and limits of satisfaction of human needs. In general terms these needs, in the context of our interaction with nature, are for living space, for energy, for substances and certain qualities that make the environment fit for human habitation.

The possibility of satisfying each of these needs on the basis of utilizing terrestrial resources is subject to certain constraints imposed by natural factors and also by socio-political conditions.

Below we shall review these constraints, and shall examine the part played by natural and social factors.

We shall proceed from general considerations of principle, without going into specific calculations, because it has been proved on the basis of historical facts that the evaluation of parameters necessary for any calculation will, with the passage of time, change fundamentally. For example, the primitive hunter judged the food resources available to his tribe by the number of mammoths that roamed the neighborhood, and not even the greatest of scientists that lived early in this century could have thought of any practical use for atomic energy, let alone thermonuclear energy.

CHAPTER ONE

THE LIMITS OF THE POSSIBLE

THE POPULATION EXPLOSION
AND POPULATION CONTROL

One of the main causes of concern about the future of humanity is the growth of the world population. Increase in per capita consumption of all the resources of our planet, corresponding growth in production output and, consequently, mounting pressure on the natural environment have created many problems which can no longer be ignored.

Thomas Malthus, as is known, was among the first to believe that available natural resources could not satisfy the needs of the growing population, that the fertility of the soil was diminishing in relation to the growth of human requirements. His name is often mentioned in literature, but very few people have a first-hand knowledge of his works. Therefore I shall permit myself to quote a passage from Malthus's once sensational book *An Essay on the Principle of Population*.

> It is an evident truth that, whatever may be the rate of increase in the means of subsistence, the increase of population must be limited by it, at least after the food has once been divided into the smallest shares that will support life. All the children born, beyond what would be required to keep up the population to this level, must necessarily perish, unless room be made for them by the deaths of grown persons....(47)

Malthus wrote that at the end of the 18th century; his ideas have many followers today. This is what our contemporary, Dr. H. Fairchild wrote in his book *The Prodigal Century* (28), published in 1950:

> But never at any times, by the most diligent employment of his inventive faculties, was man able to improve the techniques of production fast enough to take care of the natural, biological increase of his numbers. Always and everywhere the pressure of population on the food supplies produced hunger, misery, conflict, suffering and eventually death.

Overpopulation has been the chronic state of society practically all over the world during the entire span of human existence down to the last few generations.

And this is what Garrett Hardin, a noted American scientist, wrote in *The Relevant Scientist,* back in 1971:

It is unlikely that civilization and dignity can survive everywhere; but better in a few places than in none. Fortunate minorities must act as the trustees of a civilization that is threatened by uniformed good intentions.

Of course, not all proponents of Malthusian views are so categorical in their pronouncements. For example, the well-known British researcher Lord Ritchie-Calder in the article "Mortgaging the Old Homestead", published in *Foreign Affairs,* does not say outright that disease and famine are necessary or desirable for maintaining the population of the earth at a certain level. However, he lumps together the significance of the invention of the atomic bomb and of the discovery of penicillin and other effective medicinal preparations for combating many grave diseases. (24)

These medicines, says Calder, are fundamentally responsible for the present population explosion, which in their far-reaching hazardous effects can well be compared to the atomic weapon.

Such are, as Calder put it, the unexpected, unpremeditated, and at times dangerous results of the dedicated and best-intentioned work of scientists.

Thus, the unlimited growth of the population is alarming and fraught with danger, considering the limited resources of our planet.

Let us discuss more in detail the problem of population growth and its control.

Studies by many demographers have shown that, allowing for some fluctuations and occasional downturns the size of the population on the earth as a whole has, over long periods, steadily been growing. The rate of this growth has also been increasing. A clear idea of this growth is provided by the table drawn up by F. Baade. (21)

Period		Growth (in millions)		Years required to double the population
		From	To	
B.C.	7000-4500	10	20	2,500
	4500-2500	20	40	2,000
	2500-1000	40	80	1,500
	1000- 0	80	160	1,000
A.D.	0-900	160	320	900
	900-1700	320	600	800
	1700-1850	600	1,200	150
	1850-1950	1,200	2,500	100
	1950-1990	2,500	5,000 (estimated)	40

A study carried out by a team of demographers at the request of the United Nations estimates the population of the earth in the year 2000 at between 4.9 and 6.9 billion. The most realistic figure is considered to be 6.3 billion. The annual growth of the population is at present around 60-70 million.

How is this rising rate of population growth to be explained? By some natural biological causes or by the long-established tendency of people to multiply at a higher rate than that of the development of technology and culture, as the neo-Malthusians say? Neither would be correct. Nobody asserts that an increase in population is the result of certain changes in the biology of man. The real reason for the increase is a steady decline in the mortality rate and the corollary increase in life expectancy. The reduction in the mortality rate, in turn, is due to the improved standards of medical assistance, part of a general, though relative, improvement in living conditions resulting from the rising efficiency of social production, in the widest sense of its meaning.

Should the population growth continue, the resources of our planet will sooner or later run out, even if they are put to the most effective use.

But will the population continue to grow unimpeded, or will its growth be held back by some factors other than war, epidemics and famine?

Significantly, the Malthusian concept recognizes only this last group of factors and calls either for their artificial application or for a mandatory reduction in the birth rate.

There is still another factor at work: the conscious control of population growth which accords with the wishes and interests of individual families. Over the past hundred years this self-imposed family planning has become increasingly widespread.

Analyzing the growth of population the demographers have noticed that the birthrate in different countries and in different periods fluctuates under the impact of economic and social factors. Rising living and cultural standards, and growing urbanization (which means a growing proportion of the population lives in the cities), as a rule lead to a reduction in the number of births. Thus the reduction in the deathrate is offset by a reduction in the birthrate. However, in different countries the relationship of these processes has its own specifics. The reduction in the deathrate in the developing countries has, over the past several decades, outpaced the reduction in the birthrate, and this particular circumstance has apparently given most concern to the present-day neo-Malthusians.

But the main question, apparently, is whether in the future, too, the factor of self-control will be sufficiently effective to force down the growth of population below the rate of increased possibilities for satisfying its needs.

Demographers hold different views on the matter. Most demographers and other researchers in the West hold that family planning is clearly insufficient, especially in the developing countries. They urge that crash measures be taken to sharply reduce the birthrate.

Many Soviet demographers believe that improved social and economic conditions will reduce birthrates before long without drastic action on a global scale, although they, too, agree with the expedience of the family-planning programs being implemented in certain developing countries as a temporary measure. Thus Boris Urlanis (16) believes that in the present decade the birthrate has reached its peak all over the world. He believes that as early as in the 1980s this growth will begin to go down, and in the next century the size of the world population will be stabilized, i.e., the birthrate will balance the deathrate.

It is possible that things will stand precisely this way, but in our view the question of the size of population should be left open for the time being. In the future, society might have to influence an increase or decrease in population by taking certain measures. Engels wrote to Kautsky back in 1881:

> There is of course the abstract possibility that the human population will become so numerous that its further increase will have to be checked. If it should become necessary for communist society to control the production of men, just as it will have already control the production of things, then it, and it alone, will be able to do this without difficulty. (1)

In my opinion this idea expressed by Engels has fully retained its validity and relevance.

It should be noted, however, that population size and growth are by far not the only characteristics of human society in its present state and its development. In this context, the concept of population control should be viewed in broader terms.

Other characteristics that determine the specifics of the structure and the qualitative composition of society are also important.

One of them is the proportion of the population taking part in production. Is it a normal situation when a large proportion of the ablebodied population of a country cannot find use for its strength, cannot find work?

As is known, unemployment—which always exists in the capitalist countries and which at times reaches catastrophic proportions—arises not from demographic explosions but from quite definite social and economic factors.

Of no small importance is the qualitative make-up of society, the distribution of its population according to occupations, educational levels and patterns, to interests. Even when the size of the ablebodied population accords with production possibilities, the qualitative composition of the population may or may not correspond to the structure of production and to the level of technical progress.

If there is no such correspondence, then large groups of the population find no place in the social production process, and consequently no place in life. This gives rise to such phenomena as unemployment and loss of interest in any useful activity in general. The situation in many countries is evidence of this. In capitalist society today, large groups of young people have neither jobs nor a place in society in general.

One must bear in mind that at present the training of young people for jobs takes up a great deal of time and a considerable share of society's resources. With advancing technical progress, this vocational training requires more time and money.

Industrial and professional personnel must be trained with an eye to the conditions of work at our factories and offices in some 10 to 15 years from now, when the present generation of young people, who are being trained for jobs today, will be able to pay their debt to society by taking part in production.

Consequently, the training of every young man and woman about to enter adulthood must conform to a plan for the development of society, its productive forces and its mode of production. However, such a plan is possible only where there is a long-term goal and perspective for society's development.

Personnel training is given serious attention in the socialist countries, where considerable progress has been achieved in this field. The task is not only to train the required number of specialists for different industries, but also to find the correct correlation between general educational training and specialized vocational training, to combine the development of the talents and abilities of each individual man and woman with the requirements of social production.

If a person's abilities are to be revealed and developed on an individual basis, society must stimulate interest in those occupations which more than any others meet the requirements of its economy. With the development of socialist society, as can be seen from the experiences of the Soviet Union and other socialist countries, the educational standard of all its members is rising rapidly, which facilitates specialization and at the same time makes it possible to change the character of labor.

In socialist society, everyone of its members is provided with work that accords with his interests and abilities and at the same time serves the needs of social production.

In the socialist countries such regulation is the concern of the state, which seeks to ensure maximum satisfaction of people's material and spiritual requirements, including one's inherent requirement to do interesting work. Each member of society has the guaranteed right to work, to free education, to rest and leisure and medical care, to all that is necessary for a life worthy of a human being. At the same time, every person must work in accordance with the needs of society and in accordance with his abilities.

A society which has no long-term goals and perspectives cannot systematically and rationally regulate its own development, including the qualitative and quantitative composition of its population. Such a society sets no goal of this sort for itself.

It is for this reason, apparently, that many Western researchers tend to reduce the problem of overall regulation of the development of society to restricting the size of its population, regarding that as a universal remedy for all social and economic ills that society may have now and in the future.

Moreover, birth control, in their view, must take the form of compulsory quotas handed down from above.

It must also be borne in mind that all talk about the population explosion is more often than not designed to camouflage the real socio-political causes of famine and the general backwardness of the population in certain countries. Pedro Antonio Saad, General Secretary of the Central Committee of the Communist Party of Ecuador, in reply to the question put to him by a correspondent of the influential newspaper *El Universal*, "Are the social problems of Ecuador rooted in uncontrolled child-bearing?" said:

> A few years ago a group of students of economics and law, myself included, studied this problem. We then came to a conclusion which we subscribe to even today. It is true that every year the population of Ecuador increases by 3.4 percent. But Ecuador would have enough land to support a population 4-5 times as big as now, if all of it were used scientifically.
>
> The very fact that this problem has been raised and "birth control" touted as the right means of solving this problem, is but a ruse to mechanistically transpose the problems of other countries onto our soil. One must not forget that the future we are fighting for (that is, when freedom and social progress become a reality) will require a large population capable of sharply raising the level of our production.

> The other thing is a stratagem designed to mislead the working masses of our country and cause them to turn off the correct road of transforming the country. (48)

The same idea was expressed by Maaza Bekele (22) (of Ethiopia) with regard to the whole of the African continent.

As we pointed out before, the question of whether or not special measures should be taken to limit the growth of the population of the world has been given no conclusive answer. It would be well to recall Engels' words that only under communism will this problem be resolved without difficulty.

Indeed, only a society in which every member understands and regards its aims as one's own can adopt recommendations on the question of population control. Such a society will be able, by the conscious effort of all its members, to take such measures on a mass scale. We can cite many examples of mass participation by young Soviet people in building industrial plants, railways and other projects of national importance. At present, thousands of volunteers, at the call of public organizations, are building a railway which will connect Lake Baikal and the Amur River in Siberia, and they have built an auto-works on the Kama River. In the past, hundreds of thousands of young people went to northern Kazakhstan to open up vast tracts of virgin land, and still earlier, back in the 1930s, young men and women formed volunteer teams that built one of the first Soviet iron and steel works at Magnitogorsk.

At some point in the history of any country, when its people espouse common goals, rally for mass voluntary action.

The size of the population cannot continue to grow indefinitely. But as to the development of humanity over centuries and millennia, the Russian scientist Konstantin Tsiolkovsky was quite right when he made this prediction:

> Mankind will not be earth-bound forever. It will, in pursuit of light and space, take the first timid steps to penetrate beyond the atmosphere and will go on to conquer all near-solar space. (20)

Today it is difficult to say for sure how people will use the resources of outer space. This is an inexhaustible subject of speculation in scientific forecasts and science fiction. In principle, however, it is possible to utilize the substance of asteroids, to construct large manned space stations and to create a livable environment on other planets. There is no use guessing about how these ventures will materialize. But even today, long before the resources of our planet have been exhausted, a trail has been blazed for long-distance space travel, and to other planets of the solar system.

It is commonly believed that only a limited number of individuals will be able to go on space missions. This, of course, is true only for the near future. By the same token, could anyone living in the early 16th century, when the first score or so of people left Europe for the newly discovered America, foresee that they would be followed by millions of settlers, and that as a result many new states would emerge, with a combined population of hundreds of millions of people? Thus, the population of the earth and the number of human beings in the distant future are, in our view, entirely different things.

Now we set ourselves the task of examining the next phase in humanity's development—within the limits of our planet and over the period of the 21st century.

What conditions are actually necessary for people's existence? The spectrum of our vital needs is very wide—from food, shelter and clothing down to our need to socialize with fellow humans, to have an education and to enjoy the arts. To illustrate, we shall concentrate only on those material and physical (or rather physiological) needs whose satisfaction is connected with the natural environment and its resources. In their more general form, these requirements can be summed up as the needs for living space, for food, for various kinds of materials and for energy. Their satisfaction depends on the use and consumption of natural resources and on definite characteristics of the environment (the composition and temperature of the air, availability and composition of water) which make the existence and activity of people possible (in the broadest terms) and comfortable (in narrower terms).

Thus it is quite possible that in the future the limits of the resources of our planet and all the elements of the natural environment may impose certain constraints on population growth and consequently on the growth of both production and consumption.

RESOURCES

We obtain food, materials and energy from available sources, with no one particular source of decisive importance satisfying our requirements.

For our nourishment we require substances that can be found in meat, but it does not have to be the mammoth meat our ancestors ate thousands of years ago. It is important to have material to make clothing, but this need not necessarily be cotton—and so on.

To satisfy our needs we use different kinds of primary materials, substances that lie close to the surface of the earth, and, of course, energy. This, however, is not an irrecoverable expenditure of material in general. In the process of our work, after a certain amount of energy has been expended, substances are transformed from one into another. With this, as we shall see later, the natural geochemical cycle on our planet changes, too.

The amount of substance that our planet loses irretrievably through human activities is negligible, and is basically connected with the production of thermonuclear and atomic energy or with the launching of spacecraft into outer space. This amount constitutes but a small portion of the total mass of substances continually being exchanged between our planet and the cosmos.

In the upper layers of the atmosphere, the planet loses several hundreds of tons of various gases to outer space every day. Meanwhile, it receives several thousands of tons of matter in the form of meteorites, meteoric dust and other particles that fall on its surface.

But, unlike matter, energy within our planet is spent irretrievably. After being used, in whatever form of work, energy is finally converted into heat, which is then dissipated throughout the environment. This in turn somewhat changes the heat balance of the earth; and further, heat is radiated into outer space.

As we mentioned before, there are renewable and nonrenewable natural resources. Not only is the total reserve of each nonrenewable natural resource being expended irrecoverably, but at the same time, each of the renewable natural resources is being consumed at a higher rate than it is renewed. Consequently, the possibility of their further utilization is also shrinking.

But does this mean that society will have fewer possibilities of satisfying its requirements, as Malthus and all his followers claimed? No, not at all. In fact, the entire history of humankind has proved the contrary, namely that these possibilities have continuously been growing, as they depend not only on the availability of individual sources of energy, but also on a second, crucial factor, that is, on how this or that source is used.

This changes the situation drastically. The natural resources which today enable man to secure rich harvests of different crops, utilize ores containing different metals, etc., existed back at the time when our ancestors procured their food by hunting and by gathering the fruits and roots of the forest. The point is, however, that in those days these natural resources just could not be used. It took hundreds of thousands of years for people to develop the appropriate modes of agricultural and industrial production.

Early in this century, Lenin said that the Malthusian

> "law of diminishing returns" does not at all apply to cases in which technology is progressing and methods of production are changing; it has only an extremely relative and restricted application to conditions in which technology remains unchanged. (5)

The continually changing and improving methods of production lead to a more effective use of the same natural resources, and, in addition, draw into the production process ever newer natural resources, thus opening up essentially new possibilities of satisfying different needs of society.

With due consideration for these circumstances, let us examine the possibilities for the satisfaction of certain basic requirements of mankind.

Habitat. Our planet cannot change its size, but the possibilities for accommodating the expanding population are growing all the time.

A modern city accommodates such a large number of people as would have been impossible in a primitive community. The accommodation of such a large population in comfortable housing has been facilitated by technological progress in such vital areas as housing construction, communications, transport, food supply, etc.

There are different opinions on the advantages and shortcomings of life in large cities, compared to rural communities. But, owing to the operation of certain socio-economic factors, the proportion of the urban population in all countries is growing steadily. As for the difficulties of urban life created by air and noise pollution, etc., these are not the inevitable adjuncts of a large densely populated city, but rather are the result of various socio-economic and technical factors that can be eliminated.

It has become possible to build large cities in places which were previously considered unfit for human habitation. For example, so large a city as Norilsk (population about 200,000) has been in existence for more than twenty years in the tundra within the Arctic Circle, whereas some 70 or 100 years ago a community like this would have been unthinkable.

It is difficult to say what population density is considered optimal, or at least acceptable, for there are no objective criteria for this based on the biological characteristics of the human organism similar to the criteria which have been developed for food or for the microclimate of the human environment. Differences in the social and historical development of various countries have resulted in a tremendous difference in the density of their populations. In Belgium, the Netherlands and Japan, people feel no discomfort in spite of the fact that population density in their countries is 300 times as great as that in Australia (where it is 1.5 person per square kilometer). In living standards, life expectancy, and health, the Australians in no way differ from those of the Belgians, the Dutch and the Japanese. But, as is well known, there are other problems in each of these countries which have nothing to do with population density. For example, congestion in Singapore, about 3,600 people per sq km, is clearly excessive.

It is difficult to say exactly what population could be accommodated on our planet at the present level of municipal services, communications, etc., without a damaging infringement on the established requirements and habits of modern people. But it is even more difficult to estimate the possibilities and requirements of the society of the future.

There is, naturally, a physical limit to population, determined by the size of our planet. Its upper "absolute" limit, absurdly high, has been estimated. The land surface can accommodate a population which must not exceed 10^{14} people.

But if we suggest a more realistic figure, immediately we come up against the question of how much space will be necessary and sufficient for humanity's existence in the centuries to come. And, of course this immediately raises the socio-political problem: who will establish such a "quota", and how? Therefore, today, one can make only an approximate and subjective assessment. We think Baade's estimate of about 65 billion people as the maximum population that our earth can support can be taken as the basis (so far we have been discussing only the possibility of population distribution, the sufficiency of our planet's *space resources*). This estimate arises from the fact that over half the land surface people could distribute themselves to a density as high as that in modern big cities today, leaving the other half of the land "free" for agricultural uses, for rest and recreation, etc.

Another estimate would calculate that 15-20 billion people could be distributed over the entire land surface fit for habitation (about 50 million square kilometers, according to modern concepts), if the population density were to average as high as that in Belgium, the Netherlands and Japan, i.e., about 300 to 400 people per square kilometer.

This estimate gives the lower limit of the figure we are looking for. Why? In the first place because it is based on our present ideas about the possibilities of technology and population distribution (notably, these ideas are changing, allowing for higher population density). And secondly, because a much denser population already inhabits sizeable portions of the earth, many people living in one such place all their lives. One example is the industrial zone of Japan, where the density of population equals 2,000 persons per square kilometer. Another is the north-east part of the United States.

However, owing to technical progress the potentials for distribution of people over the land surface are growing all the time.

The present density of population in large cities has not necessarily reached its limit. Buildings in our cities are growing taller and taller, and there are technically feasible projects for houses hundreds of meters tall.

It is not only the land surface that is fit for habitation. We can imagine communities situated on floating platforms in the open sea or on piles driven into its bottom, on the continental shelf. We can even imagine comfortable homes built on the ocean floor, or even under the surface of the earth.

I do not regard such ways of settlement necessary or even desirable. What I want to say, however, is that the available space on our planet is not the immutable or strictly limited resource it may well seem to be. The same amount of space can, at different levels of technology, accommodate different populations. At the present level of technological development, the land surface of our planet could accommodate no less than 30 billion people to even 40 billion people—i.e., approximately ten times the population of the earth today.

At the present rate of growth of the population its maximum size could be reached in about 100 years. The question suggests itself, will this high rate of growth continue? As a matter of fact, this is basically a social problem. The scientifically substantiated data on the connection between a rising birthrate and the rising level of cultural and economic development can give us a good reason for saying that in the future the high birthrate in some developing countries (that determine average world growth rates) will go down. If the social and economic conditions in the developing countries do not change, if their level and rate of economic development do not rise considerably, and if their current policy of family planning fails to yield the expected results (since this is improbable anyway), then these countries may face an economic crisis.

Besides considering the world population as a whole, it is also important today, and will be still more important tomorrow, to take account of local peculiarities in the distribution of the population on our planet, and of the possibility that very large numbers of people will be concentrated in certain areas, etc. Could all these phenomena and space resources in general create difficulties in the development of society in some countries and in the world at large, long before the size of the earth's population has reached its limit?

Overpopulation and congestion in immense megalopolises, the uneven distribution of production facilities over the territory, and consequently of the population, plague many countries today.

For example, in Japan, with its very high average population density (about 400 persons per square kilometer), 90 percent of the population is concentrated on 10 percent of its territory.

Thus, limited space resources on the earth have never created any major difficulties (except in a very few places on our planet) for the development and numerical growth of the population. This, however, does not mean that sometime at the end of the next century such difficulties will not emerge on a global scale, particularly if the population continues to grow at the present rate, and if the way in which population is distributed does not change fundamentally.

A society which consciously plans its development will be able to overcome these difficulties by making optimal use of space resources, and, if necessary, by appropriately limiting the size of its population.

Food. Food supplies for the growing populations of our planet are a matter of the greatest concern to all those who think about the future of mankind. With the production of food growing throughout the world, the mode of producing food has been changing, too. One such change was the transition from the gathering of fruits and the catching of small animals to true hunting. The introduction of this new more efficient mode of food production enabled human society to support a much greater population without increasing its territory and released part of its labor resources for other needs.

The next stage—the transition from hunting to stock-breeding— sharply raised the effectiveness of food production still further. Now it took only five percent of the territory to support the same number of people. The share of socially useful labor necessary for the production of the necessities of life was also much smaller than it had been before.

The transition from livestock-breeding to crop-raising again reduced by 20 times the territory necessary for the per capita production of food and reduced still further the expenditure of labor resources.

The methods of food production also changed. Farming techniques developed continuously, and the proportion of the population engaged in agriculture consequently became smaller. At present this process is particularly active in the advanced countries.

The per capita production of food (the world's average) is also increasing, although somewhat more slowly than the production of other types of goods. In the developing countries, moreover, this growth is insignificant, and at times alternates with a sharp drop.

Over the past several years, new possibilities for food production have opened up. This is due in part to the introduction of new high-yield varieties of rice and other crops.

With this seemingly satisfactory general situation in food production on earth, many countries—especially the developing countries and, in a lesser degree, some of the advanced capitalist countries—nevertheless suffer from an acute shortage of some foods. How is this accounted for?

Unlike other needs, such as a dwelling, living space, and clothes, the importance of the quality and quantity of food necessary for human survival is well known. The results of medical and physiological research have long since established the optimal norms of food-intake for people of different age groups, in different occupations, and in all climatic zones of our planet.

Consequently, the possibilities for food production and for satisfying worldwide requirements for food have been estimated, and reasons for the shortage of food, malnutrition and starvation in different parts of the globe established.

Food production depends on the natural conditions in various parts of the globe and on methods of production. It also depends, in large measure, on the economic and social factors operating in different countries, and on the existing level of technical progress.

Satisfaction of the global need for food depends, naturally, not only on the volume of its production but also on the mode of its distribution—on trade, prices and other purely social factors.

A concise review of the effects of these factors—which, incidentally, accords with the results of the research carried out by many other scholars—is given in a report in 1975 to the Club of Rome prepared by a group of scientists under the guidance of Prof. Hans Linnemann at the Institute of Economics and Social Studies of the Free University of Amsterdam. (39)

It says, among other things, that the possibilities for food production in the world today are used only to a very slight degree. Thus, of the arable land of our planet only about 41 percent is used for farming (from 17 percent in Latin America to 88 percent in Western Europe).

And, further, this arable land yields about 3-4 percent (from 13 percent in Japan to 0.8 percent in Tropical Africa) of what it could produce if the modern and progressive farming methods of agriculture in advanced countries could be introduced in all farm fields on our planet (including the application of fertilizer in sufficient quantities, pest control and soil amelioration; the use of high-yield crops, etc.). Significantly, according to other researchers, the actual production of food is not far behind (15-20 percent) its potential production.

Earlier calculations made by the World Food and Agriculture Organization showed that the progress achieved in farming, should it be extended to all countries, would be sufficient to fully satisfy not only the needs for food of the present population of the world but also the needs of a population two or even three times as large (about 10 billion).

Finally, according to some research, the actual production of food in the world is quite sufficient to satisfy the present size of its population.

> The present levels of world food production are high enough to provide everyone with an adequate diet if food were distributed equally among all people, reads Prof. Linnemann's report and continues: Hunger and starvation occur because food is distributed by and large on the basis of income or buying power; hence, levels of food consumption differ widely between countries and between people. (39, p. 4)

The same idea is projected in the State of the Planet Statement drafted recently by Dr. Alexander King on behalf of the International Federation of Institutes of Advanced Study. It reads, in part:

> The fact that there is starvation and widespread undernutrition today while food supplies are still ample demonstrates clearly that the difficulties are essentially those of distribution economics and the political system. Food is costly to produce, the hungry are poor and unable to buy it... The present world production of food is about 1,200 million tons of cereals per annum which, if evenly distributed, would allow of 330 kg. per annum per capita; the survival level is about 200 kg. per capita. (37, p. 15)

Of great importance, as many studies on this problem show, is the type of nutrition. In the advanced countries of the West, meat is consumed in increasing quantities—ultimately at the expense of food consumption in the developing countries.

In their book *Human Requirements, Supply Levels and Outer Bounds*, John and Magda Cordell McHale write that

> the further anomaly here is that food aid to the poorer regions, in the form of surplus grain, is balanced out by the animal feeds imported from them which gives the West its better diet.
>
> Much of the animal protein in the Western world, the milk, meat and eggs, is produced via livestock feeds originating in oil-seed cake from India, fish meals from Latin America, etc. This is from the regions most deficient in animal proteins. In actual world production, we produce enough animal protein for two world populations! (40, p. 57)

Similar estimates have been made in a large number of research papers that have appeared in recent years.

Of these, the estimate of world food production in the future given in the book, *Can the Earth Feed the Growing Multitudes?* by Roger Revelle (USA), merits special attention. He writes that if the gross cropped area was cultivated, using appropriate technology and irrigation techniques, it would then be possible to obtain enough food to support 100 billion people, and this amount would be abundantly sufficient to meet the full requirements of 50-60 billion people for food. (46)

In the light of these facts H. P. Fairchild's assertion (see pp. 25-26) sounds absurd. It was precisely the technology of food production which Fairchild complained about so bitterly, that has always grown sufficiently rapidly and that can fully supply the present needs of society for food.

The Marquis de Condorcet (1743-1794), mathematician and philosopher, one of the ideological leaders of the French Revolution, was a lot more farsighted when 200 years ago he wrote in his *Sketches for the Historical Picture of the Progress of Human Reason:*

> This means that it would then be possible to obtain food for more people from the same cropped areas, and also that every person on earth while investing less arduous labor would have a more balanced and better diet and thus be able to satisfy his needs more fully. (47)

If we leave these potential possibilities aside we can still see that, (judging from the works of Linnemann and other authorities), even at its present level food production could meet the requirements of the population of the earth, were its resources distributed more rationally.

Thus famine, malnutrition and poverty, which plague a large part of the population of the earth, can be explained by reasons other than shortages of natural resources in individual countries or in the world in general. The socio-political background of these calamities of mankind over the entire period of its history has been studied fundamentally in the works of Marx, Engels and Lenin.

The socio-political causes of famine were examined by Josue de Castro, Jacob Oser and Otto Rühle, as well as in some of the recent studies mentioned earlier in this account. All of them have made it quite clear that, at the present technological level, food could be produced in quantities sufficient to support a population far greater than today's, and that, with an equitable distribution of resources, the present population of the earth could have its needs for food met in full.

Hardly any other reasons, except those of a purely social character, can explain the fact that not only in the developing countries but even in as advanced a capitalist country as the United States, which produces foodstuffs in excess of its national needs, a certain section of the population suffers from chronic malnutrition.

We shall discuss later some measures planned for increasing the efficiency of agriculture, especially in the developing countries. At this point we must note, however, that they require the output of more fertilizers, more herbicides and insecticides, more tractors and farm machinery; they also require more land-improvement work, which in turn calls for the use of special machines, more fuel, etc. In other words, to increase the efficiency of agriculture means bigger capital investment, bigger inputs of materials, energy and labor in industry.

In the words of Eugene P. Odum, a leading American authority on problems of ecology,

> those who think we can upgrade the agricultural production of the so-called 'underdeveloped countries' simply by sending seeds and a few 'agricultural advisors' are tragically naive! Crops highly selected for industrialized agriculture must be accompanied by the fuel subsidies to which they are adapted! (43)

His work shows the approximate correlation of crop yields, the input of energy and industrial products (artificial fertilizers and pesticides) in India, the United States and Japan.

In Japan, farmers expend 20 times as much energy and 20 to 30 times as much artificial fertilizer and pesticides (the use of which requires more materials, water and energy) as in India in order to obtain a crop yield five times as great as in that vast country. According to Revelle, it would take $500 to $1,000 per hectare to bring uncultivated lands into agricultural use. And the cultivation of all the arable land in the tropical zone would cost $500 to $1,000 billion.

Worldwide application of up-to-date effective methods of farming, and cultivation of only high-yield crops, are among the many possibilities to considerably increase the food resources of the earth. At the same time, great food reserves in the ocean remain untapped.

We mentioned previously some of the important changes in the modes of food production in human history ranging from fruit and root-gathering to hunting, and then from livestock-breeding to land cultivation. But modern fishing, for all the diversity and novelty of the technical means used, is still a variety of hunting. Essentially, our attitude to the fish population in the world ocean does not differ from the attitude of the primitive hunter to the game in an area accessible to him.

Meanwhile, commercial fishing has hardly any room left for further expansion. For some years now, about 70 million tons of fish has been caught in the world ocean annually, while the annual increment of the commercially valuable fish population, according to ichthyologists, stays within 100 million tons. It looks as though the time has come to pass from fish-catching to fish-farming, and in fact to the cultivation of various food cultures in the ocean itself. The cultivation of some molluscs and seaweeds in coastal waters yields a sizeable proportion of the food we eat.

There are no natural or technical obstacles to the cultivation of fish throughout the world ocean. But there are many political and economic hurdles in the way of marine fish-farming which can be successful only if carried out jointly by many countries.

But what kind of joint measures to cultivate commercially valuable fishes and other biological wealth of the world ocean could be really considered when only recently Great Britain and Iceland waged an all-out "cod war" that led to a temporary severance of diplomatic relations between these two partners in a military bloc.

In future we can expect to use other forms of food production. Interesting opportunities in this respect are offered by the development of the microbiological industry, which has made considerable headway in the production of feed for animals. Production of synthetic food made from nonedibles has been proved feasible. There is reason to believe that the present low efficiency of the photosynthetic reaction, which is ultimately responsible for the formation of the entire biological mass on our planet, can be significantly increased.

Hence the conclusion that, *in principle,* it is possible to satisfy the need for food of several dozen billion people, using only the resources of the earth. This could be achieved by properly organizing an effective agriculture across the world and by increasing manyfold the output of certain industries and, consequently, by greatly increasing materials and energy expenditure for these purposes.

This is the road the Soviet Union and other socialist countries have followed in order to raise the efficiency of their agriculture.

This, or any other, alternative mode of food production in any part of the world is determined not by natural but by social and political conditions.

Materials. Much of the materials necessary for the satisfaction of the needs of people come from the mineral nonrenewable resources of the earth.

For many years now, scientists have been trying to estimate the overall reserves of mineral wealth on our planet and to predict the time when they will ultimately be exhausted. For example, one of the forecasts with regard to the utilization of mineral resources was made by W. and E. Woytinsky in the United States in 1955. According to this forecast, the resources that were discovered prior to 1948 would, at the average per capita rate of consumption for that period, last as follows:

Reserves of	Last until
oil	1972
iron ore	2150
copper	1995
lead	1983 (57)

Since then important adjustments have had to be made in these calculations. First, the average per capita consumption of minerals, and consequently total consumption, increased. Second, the proven reserves of mineral wealth discovered since 1948 are far greater.

For example, in the 1960s oil and gas fields were discovered in northwestern Siberia and later in Alaska. Also, in many parts of the world, new large deposits of useful minerals were found.

So far the proven reserves of minerals, both per capita and worldwide, have been growing all the time. Thus, none of the earlier forecasts have been borne out.

How long will the proven reserves of mineral wealth grow? This process cannot go on indefinitely. The earth has a limited size, and consequently the volume of any mineral resource it contains is also limited. Here, however, one thing must be borne in mind, namely that geological surveys has been carried out on far from the whole of the land surface, and those done only to a depth of three or maximum five kilometers.

It has been proved over the past several years that minerals are stored in great abundance on the ocean floor and beneath it. We have every reason to expect that in the future these vast known reserves of many minerals, if not all of them, may also be augmented.

How efficiently can these reserves be utilized? In spite of the fact that oil is so valuable, only about 30 or 50 percent of its reserves can actually be extracted. Similar losses are sustained in the mining of many other minerals. It has been estimated that for every person living on earth hundreds of tons of rock are brought up to the surface annually, and only a few tons of this amount go into the making of goods and materials. By raising the efficiency of the extraction and utilization of mineral wealth, we shall save much of the valuable material that now goes to waste.

Another way is to utilize secondary raw materials. Even now a considerable part, that is 30 to 40 percent, of the metal goods we use is made of metal which has already served man in one form or another. Old newspapers and rags go into the making of paper, etc.

Even at this early stage, materials have entered a kind of circulation process, with multiple recycling of the same amount of substance that comes in different forms and is used for different purposes. Obviously, every new cycle of utilization requires a certain expenditure of energy. We must also take account of the inevitable loss, through dispersion, of a certain amount of matter to the environment.

It is worthy of note that, with technological advance, each of the substances extracted from the natural environment is used to satisfy more and more needs; and, conversely, it is becoming possible to satisfy each of these requirements in various ways.

Finally, we must keep in mind the growing possibilities for the conversion of substances in general, i.e., the possibility of making any product and any commodity from any raw material.

In the distant future this will lead ultimately to a situation in which the raw material reserves in the world will be measured in terms of the convertible mass of our planet.

It is difficult to estimate the necessary and sufficient amount of materials that we might need, although even now we can say with a fair degree of certainty that difficulties standing in the way of continued population growth, or increased per capita consumption due to shortages of materials, may develop much later than problems arising from a shortage of habitable space on our planet.

This does not mean that local difficulties will not arise. The uneven distribution of natural resources, particularly mineral wealth, results in shortages in one part of the world and over-abundance in another, even today. But such problems can be resolved and are in fact being resolved through trade.

Energy. The production of energy is growing rapidly, both per capita and in total. Even faster is the growth of potential for energy generation, determined by the available energy resources and the currently used methods of utilization.

Will there be difficulties with energy resources? Is the current energy crisis a manifestation of a conflict between the growing requirements of society and the limited amount of natural resources?

About 90 percent of the energy we use today comes from fossil fuel—oil, coal and gas, just a few percent from nuclear fuel and about five percent from hydro-resources, all of which, in the final analysis, are a transmuted stream of solar energy.

Despite the intensive utilization of oil, gas and coal, and the above forecasts, their proven reserves are increasing both overall and per capita. The colossal reserves of coal in the United States are almost untouched because this would require unjustifiably high outlays, according to investors in that country. Most of our readers know that the energy crisis is the result not of the depletion of the world reserves of energy resources but the result of a crisis in the economic relations between the capitalist and the developing (mostly Arab) countries.

It goes without saying that the reserves of oil and other types of conventional fuel are limited. Nevertheless, they are being developed, and will continue to be over centuries to come, at a much more rapid rate than other sources of energy. Uranium and thorium are used for obtaining nuclear energy, and there are almost unlimited reserves of raw material for producing thermonuclear energy. Physicists in a number of countries are moving closer and closer to the solution of the problem of utilizing thermonuclear energy for peaceful purposes; the final solution of this problem is, practically speaking, only a few years away.

Technological progress in exploration and utilization of outer space has stimulated the development of solar batteries and other means of using direct solar radiation. The efficiency of these devices is rising gradually, and production costs are going down.

Another important reserve of energy is subterranean heat. Hot subterranean water is used to heat several cities in Italy and in the Soviet Union, although the amount of water used for this purpose is infinitesimally small compared to the huge reserves that exist. There are technically feasible projects for power plants using water, or any other liquid that could absorb heat at a depth of several thousand meters and then yield it up at the surface.

There are also suggestions for special energy generators in the tropical regions of our planet, designed to exploit the 15-20°C difference there between the water temperature some 1-2 km deep inside the ocean and that at the surface.

Experimental tidal hydropower stations have been at work in the Soviet Union and France for several years. From time immemorial wind mills and water pumps have operated using the power of the wind.

Today the use of hydrogen for the production of energy is a scientific breakthrough that will have far-reaching consequences. Hydrogen is the ideal fuel, because the only product of its combustion is water, which does not pollute the environment.

Modern internal combustion engines could be run on hydrogen with but very small alterations in their design.

But to obtain hydrogen itself by, say, decomposing water, energy obtainable from other sources is needed. Until recently it was believed that such sources could be power plants operated on mineral or nuclear fuel, in much the same way as today. But recently biologists discovered a biochemical method of obtaining hydrogen, utilizing the vital activity of some microscopic seaweeds, i.e., by using solar energy. Preliminary estimates show that, given a chance to breed in unlimited numbers in a large lake, these bacteria could meet the energy needs of the whole world.

By making fuller use of natural energy resources, society could sharply increase the energy-per-man ratio. But that is only one way of raising the energy potential on earth. Another, and a very important one, is by increasing the efficiency of producing, converting and utilizing energy.

So far all our means of energy production have been rather ineffectual. Thus the generation of electric power at thermopower stations entails a loss of at least 70 percent of the chemical energy contained in the fuel. Further losses are incurred in the transmitting and utilizing electric power. Also low are the efficiency ratings of car motors and other engines which make direct use of the energy of fuel.

Last but not least, the expenditure of energy in the final stage of its utilization in the technologically advanced countries, and particularly in the United States, is nothing short of wasteful, particularly as it concerns transport and household needs. It is only now, with the energy crisis affecting more and more people in the advanced capitalist countries, that the ill effects of the excessive use of trucks at the expense of the more economical railway transport, and of insufficient heat insulation in houses, have come in for close scrutiny by both scientist and layman.

Despite all that, energy consumption per unit of industrial production is going down as the result of increasing efficiency in the production and transformation of energy in various stages. Thus, in the near future, it is expected that magnetodynamic generators with an efficiency of 50 to 60 percent will be in use. The utilization of super-conductivity will reduce the loss of energy in generation and transmission. And there are many more ways of cutting down on the waste and irrational use of energy.

Significantly, humanity has never at any stage of technological progress suffered from a shortage of energy resources. On the contrary, people have always developed some new method of obtaining energy long before restrictions on the old source were imposed due to depletion of its reserves. That is exactly how the problem stands today, and there is every reason to believe that during the next 100 to 200 years no restrictions on humankind's growth and development because of depletion of natural energy resources will even have to be considered.

At the same time, the energy problem may still create serious difficulties and may even set limits to humanity's development on earth. It is not a shortage of energy but its excessive consumption that might lead to such a situation.

As has already been noted, the existing permanent energy generators have a combined power of 10^9 kilowatts, which constitutes about 0.01-0.09 percent of the power of the solar energy that reaches the surface of our planet. It should be borne in mind that the production of each kilowatt of electricity at thermal power stations (including nuclear stations) is accompanied by the emanation of two or three additional kilowatts of heat, because of the low efficiency of heat engines, and also by the discharge into the atmosphere of great amounts of carbon dioxide and other gaseous and aerosol pollutants which come from all types of fuel except nuclear fuel. The electric power, used for any purposes, is ultimately converted into heat. The release of additional heat and the discharge of combustion products can induce hazardous environmental changes.

THE NATURAL ENVIRONMENT

The natural environment as a concept is very broad. In fact the term should stand for the entire known universe. However, in this account we shall confine ourselves to the planet Earth, and primarily to those of its parts which at present or in the near future may be affected by activities of human beings.

Far from trying to give a general description of the planet, of the various physical phenomena that take place on it, we shall dwell on some of the peculiarities of its structure, and phenomena which the reader might find interesting.

The sold body of the earth, the lithosphere, began to take shape several (5 to 6) billion years ago, primarily under the influence of the forces of gravitation. Its present structure came about as the result of the operation of the forces of gravitation of the earth's mass itself and its rotation; of the tidal movements of the seas, which in turn result from the gravitation exerted by the moon and the sun; and also as the result of the emanation of heat, possibly uneven, generated by radioactive fission. All these processes are responsible for the changes continually taking place in the lithosphere, including changes in its constituent elements. These changes in the lithosphere (continental drift, mountain formation) are very slow indeed, and their results become evident only after a lapse of hundreds of thousands or even millions of years.

At the same time, these gradual changes in the lithosphere build up mechanical stresses in small areas, or result in molten rocks causing sudden and precipitous events—earthquakes, volcanic eruptions, geysers, etc.

So far, no quantitative theory of the processes taking place in the lithosphere has been formulated, and they are objects of numerous, often antithetical hypotheses. Moreover, there is hardly a chance that people could actively interfere with these processes in the future.

The upper layers of the earth's crust, its surface and its soil, and the waters of its dry lands and ocean, and its entire atmosphere, including those of its regions that merge into near space, form the biosphere. It is called biosphere not only because it is the zone where life exists, but also because many of the processes that take place in it and determine its state are closely related to the phenomena of life. The biosphere is the very environment which affects human activities and which, in turn, is subjected to their influence.

The main source of energy of all the natural and many of the anthropogenic processes in the biosphere is solar radiation, which reaches the earth in the form of visible light and infrared radiation. This sufficiently stable stream brings to the upper limits of the earth's atmosphere 1.92 calories per square centimeter every minute (i.e., its power is 6×10^{13} kw). The clouds that cover 70 percent of the earth's surface reflect about 50 to 60 percent of this radiation back into outer space. A comparatively small part of solar radiation is absorbed by the atmosphere, which gets heated in the process, while the remaining radiation of a little over 10^{13} kilowatts reaches the earth's surface. The surface also reflects part of the radiation (snow about 80 percent, the ocean about 15 percent, the soil, forest and other elements 20 to 30 percent, and the earth's surface as a whole about 35 percent) and absorbs the rest. This absorption is accompanied by the heating of the land and the ocean and all objects on their surface. It is also accompanied by photosynthesis in plants, which is ultimately responsible for the formation of the entire biomass on our planet, by evaporation of moisture, and many other phenomena.

Heat emanating from the earth's surface is transmitted in a variety of ways to the atmosphere.

The difference in solar heat between the tropics and the polar regions, between the ocean and the land, creates the circulation of the atmosphere. It works roughly like this: air in the tropics is heated, rises high above the earth's surface, and flows into the cold polar regions, where it cools off and descends. The reverse movement, in the lower regions of the atmosphere back toward the equator is much more complicated because of the deflecting effect of the earth's rotation, as well as the existence of mountain ranges, special subsystems of atmospheric circulation between land and ocean, etc. Various types of feedback are also involved in this kind of circulation. For example, clouds form due to evaporation over a heated region and screen that region from further solar radiation. The sun-warmed waters of the ocean are transferred by currents to its different parts, thus creating new sources of heat, etc.

At the same time the entire system of atmospheric circulation maintains a certain mobile, yet stable, equilibrium. This can be judged from the stability of *climate* in any part of the world. We regard recurring atmospheric fluctuations around this fixed "normal" pattern of circulation as changes in *weather*.

Meteorological events are extremely powerful. The power released during one such occurrence, lasting about 10 hours and forming large thunderstorm clouds or hail clouds, is measured in scores of millions of kilowatts. The movement of air masses determining the weather over a territory about one thousand kilometers in diameter, and lasting several days, has a power of hundreds of millions of kilowatts.

An important element of atmospheric circulation is the circulation of moisture. About 450,000 cubic kilometers (cu km) of water evaporate from the surface of the world ocean every year. More than 300,000 cu km of moisture precipitate back into the ocean, and the remaining 100,000 cu km precipitate over the continents and feed rivers. It should be added as a characterization of moisture circulation that the atmosphere at any given moment contains 14,000 cu km of water, all the rivers—1,200 cu km, the lakes—280,000 cu km, all living organisms—about 10,000 cu km, the world ocean—1,400,000 cu km and the glaciers—24,000 cu km.

The expenditure of energy on evaporation and release of moisture during condensation constitutes a substantial part of the energy balance of the atmosphere.

Certain features of climate and terrain, the condition of surface water and soil determine the biogeocenosis of every region of the world. On the other hand, the association of living organisms, the biota [the flora and fauna], if viewed over long periods of time, play a part in creating rock and soil, alters the composition of the atmosphere and hydrosphere, and affect the climate and structure of the planet's biosphere.

In the process of photosynthesis, solar energy and substances on the earth's surface yield about 180 billion tons of vegetable biomass (in dry weight) and about 300 billion tons of oxygen. The plants absorb and evaporate about 30 thousand cu km of water, that is, about 50 percent of the entire water evaporating from the land surface.*

The relative contribution of the basic elements of the biosphere to the creation of the biomass can very roughly be shown as follows:

---

* Most of the solar energy absorbed by plants is expended in transpiration and only a small percentage of it in photosynthesis.

the world ocean, with a total surface area of almost 360 million sq km 43%

the tropical forests with an area of about 10 million sq km 29%

meadows and grassland (approximately 42 million sq km) 10%

the forests of the temperate zone (about 25 million sq km) 10%

farmland (about 14 million sq km) 8%

The biomass provides food for the entire animal world, including humans. The oxygen produced by plants makes up for that removed from the atmosphere by the living organisms which breathe it (except for anaerobic organisms which constitute a negligible part of life on earth), and also that used up in the processes of oxidation in the inanimate world.

The top regions of the biosphere—the higher layers of the atmosphere that gradually merge into near space—have but very little matter. The photochemical and electromagnetic processes taking place in this zone consume negligible amounts of energy compared to the forces operating in the terrestrial regions of the biosphere. Nevertheless, these processes are also of essential importance.

As noted above, the greatest part of solar energy comes to the earth as visible light and in the near region of the infrared range. A relatively insignificant part of solar energy falls as ultraviolet, X-ray and gamma-ray radiation and in streams of atoms and atomic particles. Unlike visible light, this part of the stream of solar energy and matter is highly variable. The radiation of the invisible stream of solar energy is largely the result of various phenomena known by the collective term "solar activity". This includes the formation of sun spots, protuberances and other processes.

These streams of energy and matter do not reach the earth's surface. Some of them are charged atomic particles which are arrested by the magnetic field of the earth and are accumulated in the so-called radiation belts, and others cause ionization of the atmosphere at altitudes ranging from forty to hundreds of kilometers, creating what is known as the ionosphere. Consisting of several layers of ionized air the ionosphere repeatedly reflects the short radio waves, making possible radio communication over long distances. Ultraviolet radiation forms ozone in the atmosphere, a gas which reaches maximum concentration at an altitude of about 30 kilometers. Ozone serves as a kind of screen that protects the earth's surface from excessive ultraviolet radiation, which is harmful to all living things.

The entire structure of the atmosphere's upper regions is affected by precisely these unstable forms of solar radiation. Connected with these are magnetic storms, the polar auroras, disturbances in radio communication, and other phenomena. These unstable forms of solar radiation directly or indirectly affect the lower regions of the atmosphere, and possibly the condition of living beings.

We have mentioned only some of the best known processes operating in the biosphere. All of them, just as millions of other lesser known phenomena, are interconnected in a wide variety of ways, sometimes in a most surprising fashion.

These interrelationships, which have been developing over a very long time, have made the entire biosphere into a very complex system, whose mobile and ever-changing elements balance each other out.

This state of the biosphere is called "natural equilibrium", a term which is often used in books and articles on problems of ecology and environmental protection. Appeals to save "natural equilibrium", and numerous examples of upset equilibrium and its aftereffects, would fill many volumes.

It is true that people have always disturbed and are still disturbing the equilibrium of the natural environment and have always exerted pressure on the biosphere.

As we mentioned earlier, this influence boils down to three main forms: changing the structure of the earth's surface (ploughing the steppes, cutting down forests, land improvement, creating man-made lakes and seas, and influencing the surface water system in other ways); changing the composition of the biosphere which means in effect changing the balance and circulation of constituent substances, through extraction of minerals, creation of spoil banks, discharge of various substances into the atmosphere and into water bodies, and through changes in moisture circulation; and lastly, changing the energy balance (including the heat balance) of individual areas, and of our planet as a whole.

Each of these actions disturbs one or more elements of the complex of natural processes that has affected the environment over the last geologic epoch, one or more elements of "natural equilibrium". At present, these disturbances often go far beyond the natural fluctuations of the elements of the biosphere. Some of these changes, especially the pollution of the natural environment, are clearly detrimental to all human beings. One can assume that even today (or in the very near future), irreversible changes are taking place in the entire complex of natural processes.

Ecologists persist in their belief that the development of society (population growth, growth of production and consumption) will inevitably have negative effects on humans. These consequences, in combination with the depletion of resources, amount to what is termed an ecological crisis.

The transformation of the environment in the course of production by society is inevitable. Not only human society but in fact any form of life affects nature with its activity. The present state of our planet (the oxygenous atmosphere, the presence of sedimentary rock, etc.) came about largely under the impact of organic life.

How should we regard the disturbance of natural equilibrium caused by the spread of plant life—as a progressive phenomenon, or as a degradation of the environment? If judged in terms of life in its present form, the emergence of the oxygenous atmosphere is a positive development.

The British astrophysicist James Jeans expressed the view in his book, *The Stars in Their Courses* (1931) (36), that life in the universe is something abnormal, as a kind of disease of aging matter. He also said that lower temperature, reduced intensity of radiation, and weaker chemical reactions all go to show that the matter of our planet is getting senile. But it was precisely in those early days of our planet's existence, when the natural environment was relatively stable, that life could emerge and develop. If we followed Jeans's view on this point, we would have to regard the transformation of the natural environment through vital activity, just as much as the development of life itself, as something negative. However, there are not many of us who seriously believe that this is so.

On the other hand, if we regard the development of life as a "legitimate" and positive process, then the changes which to this day stimulate its progressive development, must be regarded as beneficial.

The crux of the matter probably lies in equilibrium itself, which is the result of geological and climatic processes and of the biological evolution that took place long before the emergence of people. In other words, natural equilibrium was disturbed at the time when humans found themselves outside the pale of biological evolution.

Indeed, it is precisely the social development of human society, which is the highest form of vital activity, that has most vigorously stimulated changes in the manner of interaction between humans and the environment, with far-reaching consequences for the latter. However, this is one of the features that distinguish people from animals and plants.

It would be useless to try to restore the natural balance that existed at the time when human society was still in an embrionic stage. But it would be just as pointless to demand, without rejecting the development and expansion of mankind, that the natural balance should be preserved, unless we consider that man's only goal in life is to guard and conserve the natural environment in its pristine state.

I doubt that anyone would object to the extermination of field pests and some other living creatures which are harmful to man, or to the reclamation of land from swamps and deserts. But a question arises: do human beings harm themselves by acting upon their natural environment? Most of the ecologists are of the opinion that this is exactly the case. I do not subscribe to this view, for the following reason: if our ancestors had turned the whole of our planet into a well-cared-for nature preserve about 300 to 500 years ago (when they began their massive onslaught on nature), then modern society would not be able to exist.

Strictly speaking, the balance of nature is beneficial only to primitive tribes, since they live by hunting and by gathering fruits and berries and that only if their numbers remain unchanged.

The existence of all the other forms of social organization, including population growth and rising living standards, inevitably entails transformation of the environment in the regions of human habitation. Cutting down forests, plowing up steppelands and turning them into farm fields and plantations, ameliorating land, building new cities, organizing industrial production, and many other things that inevitably affect the state of the environment, were logical and necessary if society was to develop at all. On the whole, all these measures have helped nature to increase the production of various substances and materials, such as certain elements of the biomass without which man would not be able to exist.

On the credit side, it is necessary to have wildlife preserves set up in different parts of the world where natural scenery is not affected by people's activities and where the biocenosis, that is, the ecological balance, typical of a particular region is maintained and closely guarded. This is important not only for the purpose of research but also for the preservation of the genetic fund of our planet's biota. A great deal of work must be done to preserve all species of animals and plants, and to maintain them in sufficient numbers so as to perpetuate their existence.

It is also necessary to have parks and other nature zones that are not open to economic exploitation, and are used for the purposes of recreation, education or sport. However, it would be wrong to try to transform the entire natural scenery of our planet into a nature preserve.

Although basically human activities affecting nature have been a legitimate and a positive process, there have been many cases of action having a negative effect on the natural environment, such as wholesale extermination of some animal species through uncontrolled hunting; the disintegration of soil through the misuse of the land, mostly because of crippling one-crop cultivation and overgrazing; and the destruction of forests which play a major role in preserving our water resources. Another major side effect of our interference with the environment is the pollution of the atmosphere, the rivers, the seas, the world ocean and the soil, creating grave health hazards. Press reports and books abound in descriptions and studies of this sort.

Are these adverse effects of man's interference with the natural environment inevitable concomitants of the population growth and the development of production, as is asserted in many ecological studies? Will they create an obstacle to the development of society? Is technical progress to blame for the pollution of the natural environment?

It is true that many technological processes and new types of production introduced in the chemical industry (production of synthetic fibre, detergents, chemical fertilizers, petroleum products, etc.) have sharply intensified the pollution of the environment in industrially advanced countries. On the other hand, the same technological progress creates many opportunities to prevent environmental pollution. To prevent the discharge of pollutants into the atmosphere, the rivers and the sea, new and efficient waste-treatment facilities have been designed and put into service, though as yet on a very limited scale. An illustration of this is provided by the purifying installations used at the pulp-and-paper mill on Lake Baikal in the USSR.

An elaborate system of radioactive waste decontamination and disposal has long been in operation at all USSR plants which produce and use nuclear fuel. In fact, the great danger of radioactive contamination and the attention given to its prevention have made nuclear power production practically the cleanest and safest of all.

However, purification is not the only, and in fact, not even the principal method of preventing pollution. Technical progress has long since made it possible to completely utilize all substances involved in any technological process. There must be no waste in whatever form. This basic social need is dictated not only by considerations of cleanliness but also by considerations of efficiency of production, and rational utilization of all resources.

Scientific and technical solutions to such problems have either been found or are being sought. "Clean" and "dry" production methods that require but little water have been implemented in the pulp-and-paper industry, in the extraction of useful elements from polymetallic ores, and in the practically complete utilization of timber in storing and treatment operations. And sulfuric acid has long been produced from sulfur dioxide (a by-product of cellulose treatment).

A great deal of progress has been achieved in developing various biological methods of exterminating agricultural pests, to replace those of the chemical preparations that kill off all living things. The progress made in this direction inspires confidence that the natural environment can be protected from industrial pollution.

The main problem is a financial one, because the remodelling of industry to obtain ecological purity in production processes requires very large investments, comparable to the military budgets of the technologically advanced nations over a period of five to seven years. According to Barry Commoner, the United States would require about $600 billion to effect such transformations.

Now, whether or not society is actually prepared to spend that much money for such ends is a purely sociological question.

In the future, however, humankind will face the difficult problem of having to neutralize the effects of the energy which it generates and consumes on the heat balance of our planet, and eventually on its climate. The production of energy at thermal power plants at present and over the coming decades will account for the greatest share of carbon dioxide discharged into the atmosphere through man's economic activity. Carbon dioxide which reduces atmospheric transparency for the long-wave infrared region of the spectrum and consequently decreases radiation of the earth's heat into outer space, thereby intensifying the so-called greenhouse effect.

Methods of arresting and fixing carbon dioxide and preventing it from being discharged into the atmosphere can be conceived and put to work. It must also be taken into account that the atomic and thermonuclear sources of energy discharge no carbon dioxide. Consequently, there will be less carbon dioxide discharged into the atmosphere when nuclear power plants gradually take over power production.

But whatever its source, energy will still be consumed in large quantities. The utilization of mineral fuels, of atomic and thermonuclear reactions increases the number of heat sources in the world, especially in areas with a large concentration of industry and in large populated centres. And this changes both the geographical distribution of heated regions and also the heat balance on our planet as a whole.

The utilization of solar energy in any amounts directly from the sun would not alter the heat balance as a whole, although it would make changes in the geography of hotter and colder regions. This also applies to the utilization of the hydroenergy of rivers or temperature differences in oceanic depths and on surfaces.

Changes in the heat balance would cause climatic changes. It is sometimes thought that these climatic changes will consist in a rise in the average temperature of the lower atmospheric layers, which might lead to such dangerous consequences as the melting of the glaciers in Greenland and Antarctica, and a corollary rise in the level of the world ocean. Incidentally, such a rise—to within 60 meters—would flood vast, thickly populated territories of many countries.

One might think that a steady rise in the temperature of the lowest atmospheric regions by about 1-2°C on the whole of our planet would cause the icecaps and glaciers to recede markedly and the level of the world ocean to rise accordingly. A mere geographical redistribution of the existing sources of heat which, as we pointed out, does not change the overall heat balance, would apparently play no part in this temperature hike.

However, modern data on climate-formation processes suggest that they would, most likely, develop in a more complicated manner. The involved pattern of atmospheric circulation and the system of oceanic currents connected with it form a scheme all of whose constituent elements are in flux. As long as these fluctuations do not exceed certain limits of magnitude and duration, the whole system continues in a state of mobile equilibrium. But any considerable deviation in any of these elements from its normal state would cause an immediate change. For example, an increase in the amounts of warm water brought by the Gulf Stream to the Arctic Ocean would ultimately reduce the size of the ice cover there. And this, in turn, would affect heat exchange between atmosphere and ocean and atmospheric circulation itself.

Thus, a warming up of the Arctic climate would narrow the difference between the temperature in that area and the temperature of the equatorial zone; and this in turn might weaken the latitudinal easterly air currents and reduce the amounts of moisture thus carried from the Atlantic Ocean to Europe, and consequently might lead to a reduction in precipitation over Europe.

Most probably, the phenomena in the chain of events would subside and their energy would gradually disperse in the chaotic turbulent movements in the atmosphere and in the ocean. But at some point there could occur a reverse process—changes in atmospheric circulation could stimulate an increased transference of warm water to the Arctic Ocean. In this case, a self-sustaining reaction might set in, and even a seemingly insignificant occurrence could trigger events truly colossal compared to the initial episode.

Such self-sustaining reactions can very often be observed on a small and medium scale in meteorological processes.

Can unstable conditions play a role in climate forming processes? So far the facts at the disposal of scientists have not supported a quantitative theory of climate. Nevertheless, most scientists give a positive answer to this question, based not only on analysis of atmospheric circulation today but on the entire history of the earth's climate.

In the past the climate of our planet did change, and fundamentally at that, while in the distant past—that is, tens and hundreds of millions of years ago—climatic changes were caused by changes in the relative positions of continents and oceans, by mountain formation and by shifts in the earth's axis; climatic changes over the past tens of thousands of years—such as the last glaciation—may have been caused by other factors.

Whatever these factors, the requisite essential changes in the general circulation of the atmosphere and in the system of ocean currents can be conceived, most probably, as shifts from one state of mobile balance to another under the impact of certain trigger effects.

Among these effects may be relatively small changes in the aggregate terrestrial heat balance and a geographic redistribution of sources of heat, with the overall balance remaining unchanged.

Apropos of the geographic distribution of heat, one should bear in mind the fact that large territories are already subject to urban agglomerations, and that industrial centers and even whole countries (Belgium, for example) of hundreds of thousands of square kilometers, are powerful sources of heat radiation. For example, if Belgium were surrounded by a wall several kilometers high, the temperature of the air in that country would go up several degrees.

We devote so much attention to the question of possible climatic changes because we are convinced that these changes may be the most immediate and the most difficult barrier to the growth and development of humankind.

At present it is very difficult to say where this barrier begins, although it is very likely that even a minor temperature rise, measured in fractions of a percent, affecting the general heat balance or a redistribution of mean temperatures within several degrees over a large area (say, one million square kilometers), would set off global changes in the climate. After that these changes might proceed at different rates, depending on possible feedback.

It is worthy of note that the share of anthropogenic heat in the total heat balance will reach 1-2 percent only when the general quantity of the energy generated and consumed by humans increases roughly 100 times over the present level. Actually, this is not so much. This amount of heat would be produced on our planet if a population of 7-10 billion consumed as much energy per capita as in the United States today.

Is it possible to overcome this barrier?

Yes, it is. There are three possible solutions to this problem. One solution is to limit the production of energy. This would impose constraints on all industries and lines of production, including the production of food, and in the final analysis on the growth of the population itself, keeping its growth below the number of people that the earth could accommodate, according to the above estimate.

The second solution is to limit the production and consumption of energy on earth, and to move the most energy-intensive industries into outer space. The creation of inhabited space objects large enough for this mission will be feasible in several decades. This would make it necessary to send into outer space at orbital velocity tremendous amounts of raw material. Such operations might require even greater energy consumption. However, there is raw material in outer space, too, so why not utilize the matter of asteroids? It is hardly necessary to enlarge on this theme.

Nevertheless, we must not ignore the possibility, remote as it might seem.

And finally, the third possibility is to control overheating on our planet by regulating the climate, either by altering the heat balance or by suitably redistributing the sources of heat on its surface. We shall return to this problem later in this book.

THE VOLUME OF THE EARTH

Over the entire period of recorded history human beings have systematically increased the per capita production of food, of various kinds of materials, of housing and of energy. We have always had the potential for producing a lot more materials of all kinds than is actually needed. This potential could become a reality if the means of production in some of the advanced countries were used wherever necessary, and if the social and economic system of distribution of products, especially food, were operated with an eye to satisfying the real needs of people and not in the interests of the profit-seeking owners of resources and means of production.

The natural resources necessary for production, both real and potential, have always been available in sufficient quantities in most countries and on our planet as a whole. The land surface of the globe still has enough room for accommodating a population far larger than its present size.

People's needs, as we said before, can be rather clearly defined with regard to food, but it is far more difficult to say what their requirements are as to living space, clothes, household goods, etc. Therefore, one cannot say to what extent such requirements of the earth's population could be satisfied in the future. On the other hand, we believe, in contrast to the Malthusians, that the potential for satisfying these and other of humanity's basic requirements has always grown and will continue to grow at a more rapid rate than that of population growth.

This is a specific feature of human society. Only people can at will systematically modify the basic elements of their interaction with the environment—in other words, to change the means of production in the broadest sense of the term.

"Malthusian blind alleys" could emerge at any stage of humankind's development, if there were no technological progress and if the modes of production did not change. Neither the present population nor even the smaller population of the past would be able to support themselves by hunting, as their ancestors did. Such blind alleys and catastrophes occur from time to time in the biosphere because of the proliferation of organisms in their habitat, while the amount of the resources to be used remains unchanged. The balance thus disturbed can be restored only through a reduction of the population of this species—in other words, if they die out or migrate to another habitat. Animals and plants cannot change the nature of their relationship with the environment, cannot increase the effectiveness of this interaction, other than in the course of a very slow biological evolution. But this situation does not apply to human society.

Importantly, the development of new modes of production, and the possibility of using new types of resources, and new ways of obtaining energy emerge before the earlier possibilities have been exhausted. And this happens because humans acquire the ability to convert one substance into another, to obtain the materials they want from novel sources, long before the lack of some particular type of raw material can create difficulties for society's development.

In the works of Forrester, Meadows, Mesarovic, Commoner, Falk and many other authors, the aggregate of natural resources that can satisfy all the needs of humanity is viewed as a quantity that diminishes from a certain initial value. They reckon with the fact that the rising efficiency of new modes of production can slow down this recession. They also agree that something should be added to the initial value (now known) since new deposits of mineral wealth are discovered.

However, we find their general approach unacceptable. It is not a question of how accurate is our knowledge about natural resources, or of how accurate is our evaluation of the discovered resources, nor the question of making more effective use of a particular natural resource. What we have in mind is the fact that humanity systematically develops essentially new possibilities for satisfying its needs. And we have no grounds to think that this process will not continue in the future.

Similar ideas are gaining ground in the works of some Western scientists.

In the preface to the book *Human Requirements, Supply Levels and Outer Bounds* by J. McHale and M. McHale, the American ecologist Harlan Cleveland writes:

> None of us really knows the outer limits of the only biosphere we inhabit together. They are inherently unknowable, because they depend mostly on what we the people do in moving toward them. The 'outer limits' of any resource are essentially determined by our definition of the resource, our perception of how much of it exists (only God knows for sure), our decisions about how much we really need, how much it is worthwhile to get at, how much we can re-use, and what other resources we can use instead. (40, p. V)

Thus the possibility of providing the people living on earth with resources it has—in other words the potential "capacity" of our planet—is not a constant quantity. Since this capacity is associated with the modes of production, it is growing all the time. So far, the growth of production has been somewhat ahead of population growth. It stands to reason that this cannot continue indefinitely. The capacity of the earth has absolute limits defined by the size of the planet, also by the share or the total volume of its substance available for use, and by certain characteristics of its natural environment. It may also have some temporary, relative constraints, which would emerge if people's capacity for transforming substances were, over a certain period, to lag behind the rate of depletion of a particular resource.

Now, what type of natural resources and what characteristics of the natural environment may soonest of all create difficulties for the growth of population on earth?

It might well be the limitation of habitable space. Let us hope that people will be aware of this limitation not at the time when any further increase in population density will be near-catastrophic, but when society will be capable of consciously planning its own development, establishing a certain "quota" of space necessary and sufficient for the normal existence of the human species, and developing and systematically implementing measures to maintain its numbers at an optimal level.

Another serious obstacle will be the upper limit of the amount of energy obtained and consumed on earth.

Some other natural characteristics or resources of our planet may create considerable problems from time to time. These problems can be overcome, even anticipated, in a society which will have at its disposal the entire complex of natural resources of our planet, and which will be able to make rational use of them.

Such a society will have great possibilities for development, including possibilities for supporting a growing population.

The natural conditions we spoke of above can, it seems, ensure the existence of approximately ten times the present population of the earth. It is necessary to note here that our estimates are based on the currently held view determined by the present stage of development of productive forces and in particular by the present level of scientific and technical progress. With time, these estimates will certainly change. The question is in what direction? There is no need to guess. In our opinion, A. Clarke is right when he cautioned against overestimating our own knowledge and possibilities compared to those which the next generation will have. (25)

Speaking of natural resources or of the need to neutralize the negative impact people have on the environment, we pointed out the possibilities afforded by the available planet's resources and the present efficient methods of their utilization. The capabilities of a specific country may differ substantially from the maximum or even average possibilities available to mankind as a whole. Most of the population of the earth cannot to this day satisfy their essential needs, while hundreds of millions of people are starving. However, the explanation for this should not be looked for in the constraints imposed by nature.

In their book *Human Requirements, Supply Levels and Outer Bounds* John McHale and Magda McHale write:

> The carrying capacity of the biosphere has not been computed with any exactitude. Various estimates exist, but few indicate immediately critical global imbalances. Many pro-

vide evidence of local and regional deterioration of atmospheric, water and land use systems at critical levels impinging up human activities.

But all of these still come within our control capabilities—if suitably exercised. Given the perception of their critical nature, and of the wasteful and inefficient character of most of waste-disposal and pollutant-control systems, there are no biospheric capacity barriers to meeting the material requirements of a doubled human population in the next thirty years.

The barriers, and the dangers, rest with the range of socio-economic and political policies which govern our actions rather than being inherently a part of the human impact on the environment per se. We may set both the bounds and the amount of impact. (40, p. 80)

In other words, in order to make use of the tremendous resources and all the potentialities of our planet, and direct these resources to the satisfaction of the needs of the entire population of the earth, it is necessary to assure rational utilization of natural resources (with the use of effective production methods) and to prevent the occurrence of undesirable modifications of the natural environment. In short, it is necessary to assure a certain rational optimal interaction between human beings and the natural environment.

But all the authors whose works have been quoted from in this book are of the opinion that humanity as a whole is still very far from being able to make rational use of natural resources, from being thrifty in its attitude to the natural environment. Why is this so?

CHAPTER TWO

FROM IRRATIONAL TO OPTIMAL INTERACTION BETWEEN MAN AND NATURE

THE ROOTS OF THE IRRATIONAL

M any authors are of the opinion that human society is intrinsically antithetic to nature. For example, Lord Ritchie-Calder wrote that

past civilisations are buried in the graveyards of their own mistakes, but as each died of its greed, its carelessness or its effeteness, another took its place. (24)

Calder cites examples of what he called "irrational actions" of our global civilization which were dictated by greed or were the result of ignorance, and warns about their serious conces- quences. He calls for action in order to forestall this danger.

Man has always destroyed and is still destroying nature, writes a well-known Swiss scientist Jean Dorst:

The balance of nature began to be disturbed with the descent of man. Of course it is difficult to blame our dis- tant ancestors for willfully changing the environment in order to scratch out an existence for themselves and for their descendants. At the same time, we must not remain silent about the fact that back in those remote days man began to wreak destruction on nature, and in this way expedited the processes of erosion and degradation of na- tural association, without gaining anything for himself through sheer mismanagement and ignorance with regard to the true meaning of the land and to the ways of mak- ing rational use of it.

The processes of degradation of the land surface have intensified in the recent periods of human history, during which large states emerged and fell apart long before the advent of the industrial civilization with its origins in Europe. It has been assumed that the degradation of nature set in at a time when the white men began to spread over the face of the earth.

Their destructive economy, and their work of plunder came up against the conservative economy of the native population of all races. These conjectures are totally wrong. There is absolutely no possibility of conserving nature and even for creating some sort of balance between man and the environment, or much less, for allowing the "noble savage" glorified by Jean-Jacques Rousseau to play his part.

The primitive societies of the pre-industrial era had exerted a negative impact on a large number of natural habitats. It is quite possible that the disappearance of some animals goes back to those days.

Thus back at the dawn of its existence mankind carried the germs of destruction and even self-destruction which assumed dramatic proportions in the later phases of its history. (27)

The well-known historian Arnold Toynbee maintains that religion played a major role in the formation of man's attitude toward the natural environment. (52) According to him, the pantheism of the ancient East, Greece and Rome promoted the understanding of the unity of nature and man, and strengthened the idea that one is as valuable as the other. Monotheism in the form of Judaism, Christianity or Islam treats man as the master of nature which God has given him in perpetual use so that he can live on and prosper. The rapid development and the dominant position of the monotheistic civilizations in the world are basic factors of the ecological crisis.

Jay W. Forrester, D. H. Meadows, M. Mesarovic and many other contemporary researchers believe that the basic reason for the negative influence on the natural environment—and consequently, the basic reason for an ecological crisis that might threaten humanity unless it changes the character of its development—is the intrinsic desire of humankind to expand and to grow, which implies the infinite growth of population, the infinite growth of production and consumption. Barry Commoner considers that the basic reasons behind the environmental crisis which is arising primarily from pollution, are social. He writes:

> The analysis makes it plain, I believe, that the crisis is not the outcome of a natural catastrophe or of the misdirected force of human biological activities. The earth is polluted neither because man is some kind of especially dirty animal nor because there are too many of us. The fault lies with human society—with the ways in which society has elected to win, distribute, and use the wealth that has been extracted by human labor from the planet's resources. Once the social origins of the crisis become clear, we can begin to design appropriate social actions to resolve it. (26, p. 178)

Irrational utilization of natural resources and disturbance of the balance of nature, which lead to its degradation and threatens the very existence of humanity, are, according to many Western researchers, an inherent human quality, and an unavoidable result of the development of civilization, of technical progress and population growth, and according to others, the result of social factors.

Many researchers speak of irrational or predatory attitudes to the natural environment and its resources, but they fail to specify in what sense and from whose point of view they interpret the concept of "the rational use of natural resources". One gathers from the general context of their works that they imply not so much the interests of individual owners or groups of owners as the interests of a large collective of people—the population of a country or perhaps the whole of humanity.

Let's recall in this connection the words of the celebrated Russian geographer and climatologist of the last century, A. I. Voyeikov, who considered that man's impact on the natural environment, and the environmental changes that its activity leaves in its wake can be harmonious if there is "no conflict between temporary advantages of one man and the lasting advantages of the whole of society". (14)

This contradiction was clearly defined and carefully studied by Barry Commoner in the light of the development of industry and agriculture in the United States over the past several decades. He wrote:

> The costs of environmental degradation are chiefly borne not by the producer, but by society as a whole, in the form

> of "externalities". A business enterprise that pollutes the
> environment is therefore being subsidized by society; to
> this extent, the enterprise, though free, is not wholly pri-
> vate. . . . Therefore there appears to be a basic conflict be-
> tween pollution control and what is often regarded as a
> fundamental requirement of the private enterprise system—
> the continued maximisation of productivity. (26, pp.
> 268, 270)

The extensive-literature on the conservation of nature cites
a very large number of instances of destruction of natural resources, irrational and often quite unjustified interference in the
natural environment over the entire period of the existence of
human civilization.

In most cases this interference was prompted by the desires of
individual capitalists and monopolists who owed and exploited
natural resources for bigger and quicker profit, or by wars which
in the final analysis were waged for the same motives. This process
clearly was operating in the days of colonial conquests, and later,
with the development of capitalism, it assumed truly menacing
proportions.

Contrary to J. Dorst's opinion, the deterioration of the natural
environment—the depredation of natural resources—in the countries under colonial domination intensified many hundreds of times
over (if it did not virtually begin) precisely when vast territories
were colonized by the white man.

The period of great geographical discoveries was closely followed
by an orgy of colonial plunder, as tremendous territories were
seized, and whole countries, peoples, and rich native cultures were
wiped off the face of the earth.

Almost everywhere the plunder of natural resources began with
the extermination of people. For example, the population of Au-
stralian aborigines was reduced to one-tenth of its original size.
The once rich states of Central Africa sustained tremendous human losses: in two hundred years slave-owners captured and
moved out of Africa no less than 100 million people, of whom only
about one-third survived the journey to the American colonies.

According to M. Bekele (22, 42-45) the population of the whole
of Africa constituted, back in 1650, about 20 percent of the popu-

lation of the entire world. The seizure of large numbers of people and their transportation as slave labor to America, the cruel exploitation of natives in their home countries, the spread of new diseases, all served to sharply reduce Africa's population, which in 1970 stood at a mere 10 percent of the population of the world.

Incidentally, this dramatic reduction in the size of the native population never meant that those who survived began to live better, as alleged by Malthus and his followers.

The colonialists inflicted untold damage on forests, soil and the animal world. For example, the forests of equatorial Africa have shrunk to one-third of their former size, and their destruction is still continuing. According to specialists, the cutting down of many precious species of trees in the virgin tropical forests of the equatorial region around the world, unless stopped, will lead to the total destruction of the main woodlands in 20-30 years.

This is what Jacques Vignes writes about the plight of the forests in the Ivory Coast Republic today:

> The chopping down of forests carried out only by European companies has reached as much as . . . 2 million cubic meters a year, which cannot but create a host of problems and cause apprehension that the disappearance of forests might throw the climate and ecology of the country out of balance, with serious consequences for its geography. This total disappearance of the forests may well occur rather soon (in some 8-10 years). Significantly, timber accounts for 20 percent of all export earnings and covers almost the entire active balance of the trade balance. (54)

Most of the profits from cutting timber in Africa go to foreign companies.

The driving desire to make the highest profit in the shortest time was the main reason for one-crop farming in the colonies. Jean-Paul Harrya, a leading authority on tropical farming, wrote:

> The agronomy of the tropical countries, like that of other countries, was aimed at improving the quality of produce and increasing its quantity, rather than at looking for ways of making more thrifty use of the land.

> With the rare exception, every colonialist is anxious to derive profit as soon as possible and does not want to wait for tied-up capital to enable him to make long-term and fruitful utilization of the land, unaware that otherwise his business would before long wither, decline or fail altogether. (34)

It is not that the colonialist "does not understand" what he is doing. The point is that the economic incentives born of capitalism induce him to adopt this predatory method of utilization of natural resources. These incentives, in conjunction with powerful and efficient technology, led to the creation of large plantations of coffee, rubber, bananas, peanuts and other monocultures in tropical countries, and caused rapid expansion of animal husbandry.

Significantly, the capitalists did nothing to prevent the dire consequences of the changed regime of soil utilization. As a result, various forms of deterioration of the once fertile lands, and especially soil erosion, set in. As for the extermination of animals, many species were wiped out back in the days of colonization and settlement in North America, South America, Africa and Australia.

The plundering of nature, which started in the period of colonization, continues to this day by the foreign monopolies that exploit the natural wealth of economically dependent countries. Even those developing countries that have secured the right to dispose of their resources as they choose find it very difficult to make rational use of them, owing to the lack of tools, techniques and skilled personnel.

In the past, the utilization of natural wealth for profit grossly interfered with the natural environment in the advanced capitalist countries. The depletion of natural resources recently caused their governments to take certain measures to protect and utilize some of these resources more sparingly. Thus, in most countries, forest management has been regularized; tree cutting has been slowed down, enabling natural forest seeding and artificial regeneration. Work has been started on fish reproduction in rivers, hunting of some wildlife species has been restricted and the more valuable species of game are bred at special farms. In addition, wildlife reserves are being set up, and measures have been taken to prevent soil erosion.

However, these measures taken in some countries have run into difficulties because of private ownership of land, forests and other natural resources. The conflict between the interests of individual owners and society has become particularly evident in the context of present environmental pollution.

The owner of a factory which pollutes the air, or the water in a river, is not at all interested in the purification of industrial effluent, for this entails additional outlays that take a bite out of his profits, making him less competitive, especially if other factories in a given country produce the same line of goods or, with the emergence of multinational corporations, factories in other countries spend less money for their production. The factory owner finds it more to his advantage to dump untreated waste products and let some other organizations (or government departments concerned with the welfare of citizens) take clean-up measures at the expense of the taxpayer. And this is exactly what factory owners in capitalist countries do today.

Water and atmospheric pollution has given cause for great concern, widely reflected in literature. The pollution of air and water is an old problem, dating back to the emergence of industry, although for a long time it was mostly of local character and noticeable only in the immediate vicinity of factories. Natural dilution and chemical decomposition of the wastes discharged into the atmosphere or flushed into rivers was quite sufficient for the water or air a short distance away from the source of pollution to become clear again.

But over the past 20 or 30 years, the pollutants discharged into the air and water by a multitude of factories can no longer be diluted sufficiently to become harmless to the population and the natural environment even a very long distance away from the source of pollution. The application of artificial fertilizers and various chemicals in agriculture and the use of detergents, have increased manyfold. All this has created a situation in which changes—sometimes the full transformation of the entire composition of substances—and the subsequent circulation of these substances in rivers and lakes, and now even in the ocean and the atmosphere, have taken the place of the limited pollution that was in the past easily controlled by the "self-purifying" process.

For example, the United States—which accounts for about 50 percent of all the pollutants discharged into the water and atmosphere—every year consumes about five billion tons of various kinds of raw materials, half of which are building materials.

All that tremendous amount of substances accumulates in the soil at an annual rate of 18 tons per hectare across the country, is washed down into the rivers and is then discharged into the atmosphere. And since every hectare of land in the United States produces about 13 tons of biological mass and about 18 tons of free oxygen a year, it turns out that the amount of substances introduced by man into the natural environment in the United States can well be compared to the mass of matter generated by nature on comparable territory.

This tremendous additional load cannot be absorbed by the natural environment without serious and at times highly unfavorable changes in the geochemical cycle.

The seas and oceans also suffer from severe pollution with industrial waste, especially the North Sea, Irish Sea, the English Channel, the Bay of Biscay, the Baltic Sea, and considerable areas in the Mediterranean off the coasts of France, Spain and Italy. The concentration of petroleum products over vast areas in some places appears to be one hundred times in excess of safety levels. Also dangerous are the concentrations of detergents, mercury, DDT and some other toxic substances.

The level of pollution of the water off the American continent is just as high. It seems that only a limited area in the central part of the Atlantic Ocean and some small areas in the Mediterranean and the Baltic are still clean.

A similar situation exists in the Pacific Ocean.

Altogether, about 6 million tons of oil (according to some estimates, 2 to 15 million tons) are dumped into the world ocean, mostly as the result of the cleaning of oil tankers. And there is still another major source of pollution of the world ocean: accidents involving tankers in coastal waters. Some accidents, in which hundreds of thousands of tons of crude oil were lost, brought pollution disaster to large coastal areas. Thus the pollution of the world ocean has become a global problem.

High levels of atmospheric pollution near cities and large industrial centers create serious health hazards. They aggravate existing diseases and cause new ones, and they increase the mortality rate. Thus, about 35 percent of the people examined in the industrial area in and around Tokyo suffer from serious pulmonary disorders due mainly to severe air pollution. In Western Europe and America atmospheric pollution is caused 50 percent by cars and 50 percent by wastes coming from heating systems and industrial enterprises. The main pollutants of the atmosphere are sulfur dioxide, carbon monoxide, various nitric oxides and many other gases, as well as smoke and soot.

As it spreads, atmospheric pollution becomes a global problem. The pollutants created by the industry of the West-European countries are picked up by air currents and spread over the territory of East-European and Scandinavian countries where local pollution loads are comparatively small, and in this way the population of these countries has to pay for the poor performance of waste-treatment facilities at the factories of their western neighbors.

In the near future the problem of atmospheric pollution may become still worse, since the movement of the masses of air does not change, while the concentrations of certain types of industrial waste are becoming so large that they cannot be diluted to negligibly small concentrations, even after traveling over distances of thousands of miles.

What has caused such rapid and dangerous growth of pollution of the natural environment?

Very instructive in this respect is the book, *The Closing Circle,* by Barry Commoner, who examined the factors that over the past 20 to 30 years have led to the pollution of the natural environment in the United States. He writes:

> In general, the growth of the United States economy since 1946 has had a surprisingly small effect on the degree to which individual needs for basic economic goods have been met. That statistical fiction, the average American, now consumes, each year, about as many calories, protein, and other foods (although somewhat less of vitamins); uses about the same amount of clothes and cleaners; occupies about the same amount of newly constructed housing;

requires about as much freight; and drinks about the same amount of beer (twenty-six gallons per capita!) as he did in 1946. However, his food is now grown on less land with much more fertilizer and pesticides than before; his clothes are more likely to be made of synthetic fibers than of cotton or wool; he launders with synthetic detergents rather than soap; he lives and works in buildings that depend more heavily on aluminium, concrete, and plastic than on steel and lumber; the goods he uses are increasingly shipped by truck rather than rail; he drinks beer out of non-returnable bottles or cans rather than out of returnable bottles or at the tavern bar. He is more likely to live and work in air-conditioned surroundings than before. He also drives about twice as far as he did in 1946, in a heavier, car, on synthetic rather than natural rubber tires, using more gasoline per mile, containing more tetraethyl lead, fed into an engine of increased horsepower and compression ratio.

These primary changes have led to others. To provide the raw materials needed for the new synthetic fibers, pesticides, detergents, plastics, and rubber, the production of synthetic organic chemicals has also grown very rapidly. (26, pp. 144, 145, 146)

With a 40 percent growth in the population and a 6 percent growth in per capita consumption, the pollution load has increased about tenfold, or seven times over per person! Thus the principal part in the sharp increase in pollution was played not by the growth of the population or by the growing possibilities for supporting it, but by changes in the technology of production, spurred on, as Barry Commoner shows in his book, by a desire to raise efficiency of production for profit.

U Thant, the former UN Secretary General, who in the last several years of his work at the United Nations paid a great deal of attention to problems of environmental protection, wrote in a special report to this effect:

The deterioration of the human environment may thus be related to three basic causes: accelerated population growth, increased urbanization, and an expanded and efficient new technology, with their associated increase in demands for space, food and natural resources. None of these need be damaging to the environment. However, the efforts to accommodate population, to integrate technology into complex environments, to plan and control industrialization and urbanization, and to properly manage land and resources, have fallen far short of those required. In consequence, all nations of the world face dangers which in some fields and in some areas have already achieved critical proportions. (53)

Now, what obstructs the efforts that U Thant referred to in his report? Primarily it is the high cost of suitable waste-treatment facilities, combined with the indifference of the factory owners. According to American specialists, the construction of such facilities at all the industrial enterprises that need them would require $200 billion. And to retool the entire industry in the United States in line with Commoner's recommendations would cost about $ 600 billion as he himself estimated.

Private ownership of natural resources and the means of production, the utilization of these resources and these means of production for profit, and the private interests of the owners of these resources and industrial establishments—these are at the root of the gigantic waste of nature's wealth. It also explains the unjustified interference in the natural processes that goes against the interest of our and future generations.

Another factor reducing the effectiveness of the utilization of our planet's natural resources is the plunder of those natural resources that belong to all, and to no one in particular, such as the riches of the ocean.

The first to be exterminated were the most precious and at the same time the most readily available resources of the ocean: the fur seal, and later the whale, the hunting of which has now considerably exceeded the annual increment in its population. The day is not far off when the total fish catch will approach the full annual accretion of the fish population.

We know of many international agreements, quotas for whale hunting and other measures to prevent the extermination of the biological resources of the ocean, but these can become effective only in the conditions of true peaceful coexistence and close co-operation between states with different social systems.

A huge drain on the productive forces of humankind and natural resources is the satisfaction of the commercially inflated "needs" which have nothing in common with the genuine requirements of society and its individual members. The same desire for profit causes the monopolies to stimulate false requirements for certain kinds of commodities, the production of which serves their corporate interests only, even though in the final analysis the satisfaction of these requirements puts a burden on society.

Why, for instance, have the size and power of cars in the USA grown to such ridiculous proportions? Because the production of big cars yields big profits. The idea was aptly summed up by Henry Ford II, who said that minicars make miniprofits. (26, p. 264)

An excessive demand for consumer goods is stimulated by repeatedly introducing new fashions and by deliberately reducing the lifespan of goods, and by commercial advertising, which in turn absorbs tremendous resources and money.

Those are the main factors that motivate the spendthrift behavior of human beings with regard to our planet. The reasons illustrated above show that the potential for the satisfaction of humanity's needs may come in conflict with the real, practical possibilities, and that ultimately the state of the natural environment will deteriorate still further, thus hurting the interests of humankind.

These basically socio-political factors can be explained by the existence of private ownership of the means of production and resources, and by so far insufficient cooperation between countries with different social systems.

Alongside the negative effects of people's unintentional impact on the natural environment in the course of their activities in industry and agriculture, there are also intentional activities connected with the arms buildup and war preparations, and the military operations themselves, which seriously influence the natural environment. And in addition, there is the looming danger of deliberate modification of the natural environment for military and other purposes that threaten humanity itself.

THE DANGER OF WAR

Human activities have certain peculiarities which have long-range negative effects on the environment and which prevent the rational utilization of its resources. Above all others, we would like to single out the effects of war.

The arms drive and other activities which are part of war preparations consume colossal material resources, among them a tremendous amount of natural wealth, including some natural resources of which there is an acute shortage on earth. The arms drive absorbs the work of more than 20 million young people throughout the world who are both healthy and fit for any type of productive labor, and who instead serve in the armed forces, and more than 100 million people used in production for war. At least half the work being done by scientists in all countries goes into military research.

It is no less important that preparations for war have dire immediate effects on the natural environment. For some reason many Western researchers and public leaders, who attach so much importance to industrial pollution, pay very little attention to the pollution that comes with production for war. This indifference is rather odd, especially with regard to nuclear weapons testing. As the result of the series of atomic explosions in the atmosphere made by the nuclear powers in the 1950s and in the early 1960s, all living things on earth are now exposed to a level of radiation much higher than that caused by the radioactive substances always present in the natural environment.

Biologists are unanimous in their opinion that radiation causes certain specific sicknesses, lowers the resistance of the organism to disease and, by impairing the mechanism of transmission of hereditary properties, increases the number of deviations from the norm—i.e., produces various deformities in subsequent generations.

The great outcry raised by scientists and the public all over the world led to the conclusion in 1963 of the Treaty Banning Nuclear Weapon Tests in the Atmosphere, in Outer Space and Under Water. Since the cessation of nuclear tests in the atmosphere, the environmental contamination has markedly abated, and some still exists only because France and China, in spite of worldwide protests, continue to test nuclear weapons in the atmosphere. The treaty has to a certain extent limited the possibility of developing new types of nuclear weapons, because underground tests limit the character, scope and rate of implementation of scientific and technological projects.

At present, the nuclear powers have every possibility for concluding a treaty to ban nuclear weapons tests in all spheres.

As for military operations proper, they have always inflicted great damage on the natural environment, and in the final analysis, on people themselves. However, untill recently, including the period of World War II, this damage was comparable to that inflicted by industrial activities on nature. During the past 15 to 20 years the situation has changed fundamentally.

We shall not discuss here the consequences that a worldwide thermonuclear conflict might have for the natural environment, for this has been extensively treated in many books and articles. It is well known, however, that the use of nuclear weapons in a worldwide conflict would sharply, perhaps irreversibly, change the condition of the natural environment not only on the territory of belligerent nations but on most of our planet, if not all of it. And the question of whether the surviving part of humanity could exist in the changed ecological conditions is a subject for conjecture and hypotheses.

However, even without using nuclear weapons, as the sad experience of the Vietnam war has shown, military operations may trigger ecological effects on a scale comparable to those of the military operations themselves. The use of herbicides, defoliants and other chemical agents in the so-called Food Denial Program led not only to the destruction of rice fields and other crops but also to the destruction of forests over a large part of Vietnam. That undoubtedly caused a lasting disruption of the ecological regime in the whole of the country.

Yet those are but unintentional byproducts of military operations. It is feared that the development of military technology would lead to still more dangerous situations.

In September 1974, at the 24th session of the UN General Assembly, the Soviet government submitted the draft of an international agreement on the prohibition of action to modify the environment and climate for military and other purposes incompatible with the maintenance of international security, well-being and health. In his speech at the UN session, A. A. Gromyko, the Soviet Minister of Foreign Affairs, explained that existing scientific and technical innovations had made it possible to modify the conditions of the natural environment, e. g. to affect weather, within limits.

Further scientific and technological progress, as may well be expected, will make these possibilities still more extensive. In this connection, the Soviet government deems it necessary to take measures now to prevent military or any other hostile uses of science today or in the future.

Thus the question of influencing elemental natural processes (in the old days the very term "the elements" signified something over which people had no control) has for the first time become the subject of international negotiations. However, the idea of using the means of warfare as a tool to affect the natural environment and the weather, as well as the idea of preventing the advent of such new weapons, emerged much earlier.

In this connection, it is worthwhile looking through old newspapers and scientific magazines published in the United States. In 1946-1947 American scientific and public journals for the first time published reports on the successful experiments carried out by Vincent Schaefer, Bernard Vonnegut, Alexander Langmuir and other scientists to induce artificial precipitation from certain types of clouds.

The USSR and Germany had first carried out experiments of this kind before the World War II, and it was clear even at that initial stage that in principle it was possible to induce artificial rainfall. The American scientists used effective agents—dry ice and silver iodide—that stimulated crystallization of supercooled clouds and caused intensive snow and rainfall over areas of hundreds of square kilometers.

Those were very interesting and important (albeit initial and largely preliminary) results, which set in train massive research in many countries.

But there were ideas of a different kind, too.

In 1950, Prof. Wider of Cornell University proposed that some devices be installed on ships in the Atlantic to reduce rainfall in the "communist world" and thereby cause artificial drought there. (15)

In 1953, the American industrialist Harry Hugenheim, at a ceremony in which he was awarded a prize from the American Meteorological Society, said: "An atomic bomb is the greatest means of destroying life; a meteorologic war would be the greatest means of destroying the means of life themselves." He then launched into a long disquisition about using certain "substances" (!) over the Atlantic Ocean or over Western Europe to "dehydrate" the clouds on their way to Russia, or, the other way around, to stimulate torrential rain in Russia. (35)

In November 1957, Prof. Edward Teller, the father of the American hydrogen bomb, in a bid to obtain credits from the US Senate, said that if science in America did not achieve any major breakthrough, Russia would lead the world in many different areas of science and technology, leaving the United States far behind. And that, in his words, might reduce America to a second-rate power and would make her completely defenseless. In fact, he said, the Russians would then be able to make their terms without making war, especially if they learned how to control the weather or change the level of the world ocean.

It looks as if competent American scientists eventually succeeded in convincing their naive and equally bellicose colleagues that any changes in the weather on a large scale, and especially modification of the climate on a global scale would, in practical terms, require intensive international cooperation and concerted action by many countries. The hullabaloo in the press died down, while serious work at many research centers and laboratories in the United States was carried on. The results that this work produced were interesting and important. Meanwhile, the Pentagon, too, tackled weather-modification problems.

In 1974, the American government released two books in unpretentious jackets. One of them is a transcript of the hearings on the need for an international agreement prohibiting the use of environmental and geophysical modification as weapons of war, and the other the hearings before the Senate subcommittee on foreign relations on weather modification activities. (55)

Both these transcripts were made between January 25 and March 20, 1974, when the Subcommittee on Oceans and International Environment of the Committee on Foreign Relations of the US Senate met to discuss the political aspects of the environmental problem. This book was, until May 20, 1974, classified as top secret but was then declassified.

The other book is a transcript of the hearings (on September 24, 1974) before the House Subcommittee on International Organizations and Movements of the House of Representatives Committee on Foreign Affairs, on various questions relating to the signing of an international agreement prohibiting the use of weather modification as a weapon of war. (56)

The contents of both books are very interesting since prominent political figures, competent scientists and military experts took part in the discussions.

In the book on the US Senate subcommittee hearings, an introduction by Senator C. Pell states that back in 1972 many research centers and public organizations in the United States, as well as individual scientists and political leaders, considered it necessary that the US government should lead the initiative in signing an international agreement banning all the work involving the development and use of methods of modification of the natural environment for military purposes.

American scientists also moved to have this question discussed at the December 1972 Dartmouth conference of Soviet and American scientists (among them the author of this book), businessmen and political figures. Needless to say, the Soviet participants in the conference supported that move.

Finally, in February 1973, the US Senate adopted a resolution recommending that the US government initiate an international agreement to that effect. The fact that a whole year later this resolution still had not been implemented led to a discussion of this question at the Senate meeting.

The text of this document makes it clear that the failure of the US government to sign international agreements on preventing actions aimed at modifying the climate of our planet was the result of the Pentagon's determination to use the existing methods that made such modification possible as a weapon of war. And it was not merely an intention. Military experts testified at the congressional hearings that for six years the US army had staged some important experiments for inducing rain in Indochina while the war was in progress. They said that these experiments, which absorbed many millions of dollars, were meant to lengthen the season of bad roads in the area of the so-called "Ho Chi Minh Trail". The army experts believed that as the result of these measures the amount of rainfall had increased.

It is doubtful that such experiments could markedly change the meteorological conditions for any length of time, e.g., to increase the amount of rainfall by 20-30 percent over a large area. However, it is quite possible that the amount and intensity of rainfall could be increased by 10-15 percent over a comparatively limited area (several thousand square kilometers).

Many thousands of experiments conducted for peaceful purposes in different countries over the past 10-15 years have confirmed this view. It is true that such intensified rainfall could inflict serious damage on the civilian population by, say, further destroying a damaged dike and causing a flood. Hydroscopic substances used for stimulating precipitation from warm tropical clouds can also be used for corroding metal and destroying vegetation, but they can inflict sizeable damage only if used in large amounts. For this reason, these substances should really be classed as chemical weapons with a collateral meteorological action. Incidentally, radar jamming techniques can also stimulate precipitation from warm clouds.

The hearings at the House Subcommittee, which were the subject of the other book, took place after the Soviet Union had submitted its proposals on the above question at the UN General Assembly.

We hope the reader will agree that the draft agreement on the prohibition of action to modify the environment and climate for military purposes submitted by the Soviet government at the 24th UN General Assembly was both timely and relevant.

In 1976, the UN General Assembly, at its 31st session, approved the Convention on the prohibition of military or any other hostile use of environmental modification techniques and recommended that all nations sign and ratify it.

The idea of the agreement is to ban the military and other hostile use of not only such weather modification methods as intensified rainfall or dispersion of clouds and fog, which are known to us today, but also methods which may be invented in the near and distant future.

We referred above to a possible instability of some natural

processes, including meteorological phenomena. Significantly, the hydrosphere and the lithosphere from time to time also develop a state of instability, in which even a minor modifying factor can set off a large-scale process. For example, an avalanche, which can destroy villages and block a valley with snow, can be triggered by a rifle shot. A few hundred cubic meters of water which have filled a small lake high in the mountains to the brim, can cause a formidable mudflow and wipe out a large city.

There is every reason to believe that earthquakes initially are caused by small shifts and other displacements of large blocks deep underground, where they develop a state of instability. We meet with situations when even a small disturbance in the structure of the earth's surface can have far-reaching consequences. Cases are known when the extraction of sand or gravel from a beach, which had for a long time suffered no noticeable consequences, suddenly caused intensive erosion of the shore by tidal action and offshore currents. Such phenomena have caused serious damage in some places on the Black Sea coast of the Caucasus, and especially around the health resort of Pitsunda.

Throughout the entire biosphere run such tenuous, extremely elusive chains of occurrences, linking the animate and inanimate elements of the natural environment which influence one another. For example, even the slightest deviation from the normal temperature of the water causes whole populations of some commercially valuable fish to migrate hundreds and even thousands of miles away. Any slowdown in the speed of vertical currents in the ocean reduces the supply of organic substances from the deeper regions for the plankton on the surface and thus adversely affects the supply of feed for fish, cetaceans, etc.

These interconnected phenomena in the biosphere, and the processes that occur in the environment under the impact of human activity, and as a final effect, the impact of these processes on humans themselves—have become an important object of scientific inquiry. Their careful examination is necessary in order to avoid all possible negative effects of man's impact on the natural environment, and also to develop optimal forms of interaction between humans and nature, to transform nature in accordance with the needs of human society.

The peculiarities of some natural processes, and especially the emergence of instability in some of them, make it increasingly possible to deliberately influence the natural environment. This peculiarity has been used to alter meteorological conditions. (The scientific and technological aspects of weather modification will be dealt with later.)

Also noteworthy in this respect are the possibilities for modifying the conditions of the upper atmosphere. At an altitude of hundreds of kilometers from the earth's surface, the amount of matter in the atmosphere is insignificant. Also small is the energy involved in the processes that occur there. It was widely believed only a few decades ago that there was no air at such altitudes, and that therefore all the processes taking place in the void, with negligible amounts of matter or energy, were of no importance. However, our views on this outer region of the atmosphere and adjacent near space have since been changed. It has been established that the condition of the ionosphere—i.e., the ionized layers of the atmosphere that lie at altitudes ranging between 50 and 300 kilometers—variously affects the propagation of radio waves of different lengths, i.e., determines the potential for and conditions of long-range radio communication. Special services in many countries carry out observations of the ionosphere, calculate which frequencies can best be used, and send the required information to radio operators.

The atoms and charged particles ejected from the sun are captured by the magnetic field of our planet and are then concentrated in so-called radiation belts. As the result of some more violent processes taking place on the sun, the concentration and the energy of the particles in the radiation belts, and the intensity of different kinds of radiation in outer space are so high that they create a serious health hazard for astronauts. It is also feared that, in the future, passengers aboard supersonic planes that fly at high altitudes might meet with similar danger. For that reason, special services have been set up to monitor the radiation situation in outer space by collecting and processing information about the condition of the sun and the upper layers of the atmosphere, and to provide radiation forecasts for astronauts. These forecasts are just as necessary for the astronauts as weather reports are for fliers.

Thus the phenomena taking place in the upper layers of

the atmosphere have acquired great practical significance. As we just said, they involve a relatively small amount of matter and energy. This explains why they are so susceptible to any interference from outside and why they can be so easily modified, even without a "trigger effect". For instance, the first explosion of a small atom bomb in outer space, made by the United States in 1959, precipitated a whole chain of disturbances there. The explosion seemed to have injected additional atomic particles into the radiation belts and in this way increased the danger of radiation, modified the condition of the ionosphere, upset radio communications over a large area and had many other effects.

Changes in the upper layers of the atmosphere have yet another important result. The connection between solar activity and weather, i.e., the condition of the lower regions of the atmosphere has been under study for a long time. It is not quite clear how this mechanism works, although scientists are positive that such a connection does exist. Whatever this mechanism may be, it works most likely through the upper layers of the atmosphere and probably through a trigger effect, because it is hardly possible that so much matter and energy expended in the lower regions of the atmosphere can be brought into play by low solar activity directly.

If a connection between the electro-magnetic processes in the upper atmosphere and the weather in its lower regions does exist, modification of conditions in the upper layers can also serve as a method of influencing the weather.

As noted before, the climate on earth is in danger of being changed by the unintended effects of man's activity. The question arises: could man's intended actions, directed at modifying the climate, also prove dangerous? The question will be dealt with at a later stage.

Earlier we spoke primarily about various effects on meteorological and hydrological processes. Lately scientists have been devoting more and more attention to phenomena that link up the electromagnetic fields in the environment directly with the biological processes in living organisms, including the human organism. It is well known that strong electric and magnetic fields near powerful radar stations exert a harmful effect on the human body, although we may not feel them.

What can we say about the weak fields comparable to the natural magnetic and electric fields of our planet? Some scientists believe that the oscillation frequency of the terrestrial magnetic field which coincides with the oscillation frequency of the rhythms of the brain, may have certain effects on the human body. This is still arguable, of course. Nevertheless, one must bear in mind that human beings are connected with the environment in very many ways, and not all of them by far have been discovered by science. In the future, we will probably be able to induce weak oscillations in the magnetic field of a given frequency over a given area.

Great vistas are opening up in the field of genetics. Only recently we witnessed the spectacular achievements of chemists who synthetized substances which do not occur in nature, substances which have certain qualities and characteristics that they sought to impart. Now we have become used to such things. Synthetic textiles, artificial leather, strong fiber, excellent dielectrics, and many other materials that combine different properties are produced in most countries of the world.

Now it is the turn of the biologists, with the first results obtained in such sensitive areas of research as modification of the structure of the deoxyribonucleic acid which transmits hereditary properties from one generation to another.

This opens up the possibility of transforming the hereditary properties of the simplest organisms—viruses and bacteria. In time this may, on the one hand, become a marvelous means of combating harmful bacteria and hereditary diseases, but, on the other hand, it may be used to turn innocuous and even useful microorganisms in the human body into bacilli as dangerous as those that cause the plague.

Science, by the very logic of its development, has moved in a variety of ways into a new area of research, that of transforming nature itself. We can dig a giant pit, fill it with water and turn it into a man-made sea. We also can by a mere prod put to use powerful elemental forces, we can create new materials which do not occur in nature, and very possibly we shall soon create a new organism.

It is hard to imagine all the possibilities that scientific and technological progress opens up. And it was precisely to prevent these possibilities from being utilized against the interests of humanity that the Soviet government submitted, at the 30-th session of the United Nations General Assembly, a draft agreement on the prohibition of the development and manufacture of new types of weapons of mass destruction and new systems of such weapons that could be developed using the present and future achievements of science and technology.

The sad experience of the past provides abundant evidence that scientific discoveries were almost invariably used for military purposes, and were even made exclusively for war. But if we want to forestall a serious crisis, or a possible collapse of modern civilization, we must put an end to such a state of affairs.

And this is becoming possible to achieve because of the vast experience accumulated by humankind in the process of its social development.

THE ROAD TO OPTIMIZATION

We have already discussed various aspects of the irrational behavior of human beings with regard to the natural environment and its resources and the attempts to use environmental modification for military and other hostile purposes. Many examples illustrating the work being done in this field by scientists in the United States and other Western states have been cited. The reader could quite reasonably inquire about the state of things in the Soviet Union, and might want to know what socialist society has done to resolve the problem of interaction between people and nature.

This is a legitimate question which, it seems, is of interest to many people. No wonder that every year one or two books and a number of articles are published in the United States on nature conservation in the Soviet Union.

In his book, *The Spoils of Progress: Environmental Pollution in the Soviet Union,* published in the United States in 1972, M. Goldman describes the environmental situation in the area of Lake Baikal in Eastern Siberia. He writes:

> Not only are most of us unaware of environmental dis-
> ruption in a socialist country like the USSR, but somehow
> it has become a tenet of conservationist folklore that envi-
> ronmental disruption will no longer exist in a society where
> the state owns all the means of production. (31, p. 2).

In fact the entire book was written with the purpose of discred-
iting what the author calls "folklore".

Before proceeding to tell about the state of affairs in the Soviet
Union, we would like to go back to our earlier question about
the rational behavior of humans vis-à-vis nature. We referred
many times to man's irrational actions. So the question is what is
meant by the term "rational" ?

We would propose the following definition: the rational utilization of natural resources, like rational modification of the environment in the habitat of any society, is such as can best serve, on
the basis of the currently available information, the long-term
needs of society's present and future generations.

This definition can hardly be contested or objected to, for variously worded, similar definitions have already been offered in
ecological literature. The idea of this definition boils down to the
assumption that society can make rational use of the natural
environment and its resources, only if certain imperatives are
observed.

First, the very definition of "rational" or "irrational" with regard to any actions affecting nature can be applied only in a society which is not divided by conflicting interests but on the contrary is united by lasting common interests.

Second, the rational use of the natural environment requires
that society should have a long-term plan of action and should
be able to use any of its resources for implementing that plan.
This necessitates common ownership of all the environment and
natural resources in the entire zone of human habitation.

Third, society must be organized in such a way that it will have
no grounds for serious conflicts.

Socialist society fully meets these requirements; it consciously
directs its development, having clearly formulated long-term aims,
and it can and does organize rational interaction between human
beings and nature.

Such long-term goals are being carried out in the Soviet Union. It has long been known that Russia has very rich natural resources, but ironically, before the 1917 socialist revolution, even coal was shipped from Britain for the factories in Petrograd. The Soviet government showed its great concern for the national wealth of the country right after it took power in Russia. First of all, it was necessary to study the vast territory of the country, to locate and estimate the reserves of mineral wealth, to examine the system of rivers and seas. This task, viewed as one of paramount importance, was incorporated in the plan of scientific and technical work of the Academy of Sciences drafted by Lenin in 1919. (6)

The dedicated work of the first generation of Soviet scientists soon yielded good results. Rich deposits of mineral wealth and gigantic reserves of hydropower, new inland waterways and the Great Arctic Route, detailed soil maps, and numerous other discoveries and investigations provided a solid economic basis for our country's sweeping plans for economic development.

Since then the study of natural resources has been planned in the Soviet Union so as to increase their total reserve, which is necessary for a continuous development of the national economy.

Alongside the study of natural resources the Soviet government has taken systematic measures for their rational and effective use in the interests of the people, and to protect the natural environment.

In his speech "Fifty Years of Great Achievements of Socialism", Leonid Brezhnev stated the clear-cut position of the Soviet state on this question:

> The tempestuous growth of science and technology makes the eternal problem of the relationship between man and nature especially important and timely. Even the first socialists held that the bringing of man and nature closer together would be a characteristic of the future society. Centuries have passed since then. Having built a new society, we translated into reality many of the things which the predecessors of scientific socialism could only dream of. But nature has not lost for us its tremendous value both as the primary source of material wealth and as an inexhaustible

well-spring of health, happiness, love of life and the spiritual wealth of every man.

All this should be recalled to stress how important it is to treasure nature, to protect and augment its wealth. Economical, efficient use of natural resources, concern for the land, forests, rivers and pure air, for the flora and fauna—all this is our vital, communist cause. We must preserve and beautify our land for present and future generations of Soviet people.

The more rationally we utilize nature's riches, the greater the successes industry, agriculture and science will score, the higher the productivity of social labor will rise and the richer, finer and more cultured the life of the Soviet people will become. (9)

The Soviet Union has a long-term goal: to satisfy the growing material, cultural and intellectual requirements of all its citizens. A society which is equally responsible for the efficiency and required volume of production, for the health and well-being of its members, must plan and develop its economy in such a way that one goal will not stand in the way of the other.

The national economy of the Soviet Union is built in accordance with the principle of effective utilization of all available natural resources. The planning of the economy as a whole makes it possible, and obligatory, to take into consideration both immediate and long-term requirements and their consequences, thus safeguarding the interests of both present and future generations.

The entire natural wealth of the Soviet Union belongs to the whole people, and this means that no organizations or factories, or individual citizens can own land, its mineral wealth, its bodies of water, forests and other natural resources. They can use them only by permission and under control of the state.

These principles are formalized in the Constitution and in the laws based on it, including the Fundamentals of Legislation of the Union of Soviet Socialist Republics and Union Republics on health protection, on the use of land; on water management; on the use of mineral resources, and many other laws and government decisions. These legislative acts serve as the basis for taking action to make effective use of and to protect natural resources and the environment.

To illustrate. The Soviet Union has vast water resources. The total runoff of its rivers comes to about 5,000 cu km a year, or about 18,000 cu m per citizen living on its territory. But the geographical distribution of its water resources is highly uneven. In the European part of the country, where about 80 percent of the entire production is concentrated, there are but a few large rivers, with a total runoff of a mere 1,100 cu km a year—i.e., 3,000 cu m of water per person a year—which is considerably less than in the United States, China and many other countries.

The runoff of rivers in the USSR fluctuates from one year to another, and is in fact very uneven throughout the year: about 80 percent of the runoff occurs in the spring and summer months. All that calls for serious measures to change the runoff system of our rivers on a national scale, in order to optimize the use of our water resources. To achieve this purpose, General Project for comprehensive utilization of water resources has been drawn up and is a part of the still broader overall national economic development plan. Therefore, all the schemes for the use of water resources are closely tied in with the plans for the development of industry, with projects for irrigating arid land, with the available mineral resources in a given area, with the size of the population and its occupation patterns, with communications and with many other conditions.

The General Project served as the basis for regularizing the main rivers in the European part of the Soviet Union. Now large systems of water reservoirs have been set up on the Volga and the Dnieper, and giant hydroelectric stations generate colossal amounts of electricity. The high dams of these stations raised the level of water in these rivers, making irrigation of vast arid areas possible. At the same time, the entire river system of the European part of the USSR is one huge transport network, connecting the Black Sea, the Sea of Azov, the Baltic Sea, the Caspian Sea and the White Sea.

A great deal of work to transform the river network and build irrigation canals has been done in the republics of Soviet Central Asia and in Transcaucasia.

With the development of the national economy, the existing river systems are being developed and new such systems are being built. At present, a project is under consideration for diverting part of the runoff of the northern rivers—the Pechora and the Northern Dvina—into the Volga basin, in order to augment the Volga's flow and in this way maintain the present level of the Caspian Sea. The water will also be used for irrigation.

Another project that has come in for scrutiny involves the possibility of diverting part of the flow of the great rivers in Western Siberia in a southerly direction, for irrigation purposes in Kazakhstan and in the Soviet Central Asian republics.

Soviet agriculture is developing in accordance with a long-range plan. The variety of climatic conditions in different parts of the country makes it possible to support a highly diversified agriculture. But, of course, there are great difficulties to conte̶ with. For example, only one-third of the arable land in t̶ ̶ ̶et Union can yield steady harvests without re̶l̶y̶i̶n̶ ̶ ̶ ̶ ̶ ̶ ̶cial irrigation; the remaining two-t̶h̶ ̶ ̶ ̶ ̶ ̶ ̶ ̶ ̶ ̶ ̶ons of insufficient humidity that suffer̶ ̶ ̶ ̶ ̶ ̶ ̶ ̶ ̶ ̶sional droughts. In the United States, by comparison, the situation is exactly the opposite: two-thirds of the arable land has sufficient moisture and only one-third is from time to time affected by drought. There are many places in the Soviet Union with excessive humidity. Therefore, effective farming depends on good use being made of all the possibilities of irrigation and land improvement, as well as of the purely climatic characteristics and water resources of a given region.

During the tenth Five Year Economic Development Plan (1976-1980) some four million hectares of arid land was irrigated and about 5 million hectares of overhumid land was ameliorated.

Forest belts have been planted to protect crops from dust storms, to conserve moisture in the soil and retain the snow in the fields. The forests planted in the 1950s proved particularly effective in protecting farm fields in the winter of 1969, when many of our farming regions were hit by severe dust storms.

From 1976 through 1980, more than 1.4 million hectares of new field-protecting forest belts were planted. Wide strips of forest were planted on riverbanks and along deep gullies. Forests were also planted over tens of millions of hectares to strengthen and improve the topsoil. The Soviet government allocated considerable sums of money for all these purposes.

A great deal of attention is devoted to the optimal utilization of our forests. The Soviet Union has the world's biggest forest reserves. The government has set up forest protection and forest fire-fighting services, and forest restoration has been organized over a vast territory of our country.

Ore deposits are extracted from every ore basin until their reserves have been exhausted. It is worthy of note that not only are easily accessible deposits of coal and other mineral resources lying close to the surface extracted, but also the deposits which lie deep underground. For example, the coal that is extracted by open-cut mining in Siberia is very cheap compared to the coal extracted in the deep Donets basin in the Ukraine. It is quite possible that if Donets mines were capitalist-owned, they would have long been closed down. But in the Soviet Union the attitude to mineral resources and their extraction is quite different. We take into account the fuel balance of the country as a whole, the size of our population and the available manpower, and the existence of other types of fuel. With all these factors considered, it has been decided to continue the extraction of coal in the Donets basin until all its reserves have been depleted.

Methods of extracting metal from ore, as well as methods of extracting oil and natural gas, are being improved, although there is still a lot to be done in this field. Given ideal conditions, less than 50 percent of the oil discovered is eventually mined, the rest remaining underground. This situation obtains in all countries where oil has been found. Only recently, serious measures were initiated to stop the wasteful burning of associated gas during oil extraction. In many countries, billions of cubic meters of such gas are still burned up in this manner.

Efficiency in choice of materials for production is being improved. Expensive metals are being replaced wherever possible by less expensive plastics, concrete, etc.

Re-use of materials for the second time, and even multiple re-use, are gradually becoming a standard technique in saving resources and reducing environmental pollution from waste.

Despite the fact that in the Soviet Union environmental pollution is mostly of local character and not nearly as extensive as in other technically advanced countries, the problem of purification and prevention of discharge of wastes is regarded as one of the most important, considering the rapid development of the national economy. No factory can be started up without appropriate purifying installations. Waste-treatment facilities are also being installed, although not nearly as rapidly as we would like to see them, at old enterprises built during the last war or in the difficult period immediately after it.

Thanks to these measures, the percentage of water recovered from waste is growing, in spite of the rapid development of industry and the increasing amount of industrial waste. Thus, over the past seven years the amount of recycled water in the total amount of effluent has grown from 43 to 65 percent.

In March 1972, the Central Committee of the CPSU and the Council of Ministers of the USSR decreed stern measures to clean the Volga and the Urals. Concentrated in the Volga basin are large numbers of diverse industrial establishments, many of which were built a long time ago and therefore have no proper waste-treatment facilities.

Some of these measures have been enforced. Large waste-treatment plants have been built in the city of Gorky, a major industrial center on the Volga.

Special measures are being worked out to protect the more valuable bodies of water. Conservation of the waters of Lake Baikal is a case in point. To protect the purity of water in this unique lake has become the concern of the whole nation. The problem of Lake Baikal has been discussed by specialists and given much prominence in the press.

Discussion of the Baikal problem appeared in the foreign press, too. In his book, M. Goldman attempted to prove that the measures being taken by the Soviet government to protect Lake Baikal were just as inadequate as similar measures being taken in the capitalist countries. He wrote:

> Unfortunately the rape of Lake Baikal shows that public greed and lust can be as destructive as private greed and lust. (31, p. 208)

However, facts must also be considered. The government's decrees outlined the objectives of the Soviet state with regard to the Baikal area: to protect this unique natural complex and, at the same time, without disturbing its main characteristics, to carry on the exploitation of the natural resources of this area. Acting strictly in accordance with this goal, the appropriate organizations drew up a comprehensive program of economic development not only for the lake itself and its coastal regions but in fact for the entire Baikal basin. The plan is now being successfully carried out.

To begin with, appropriate measures were taken to preclude any direct adverse influence on the ecological character of Lake Baikal. The factories built on the shores of the lake were fitted with special purifying facilities, combining mechanical, chemical, and biological methods of purification, which are most probably the best in the world. The cost of these purifying installations is close to a quarter of the cost of the factories themselves. These installations have brought down the level of particulate matter in the factories' effluent below the maximum permissible concentrations adopted by the sanitary and fish-protection services. Mr. Russell E. Train, Administrator of the Environmental Protection Agency, whom the author of this book invited to visit the Baikal area back in 1972, was very favorably impressed by the efficiency of these installations, as can be judged by his articles in the American press.

At present, work is nearing completion on the building of purifying installations at factories in the middle reaches of the River Selenga and some other tributaries of Lake Baikal. In fact, the entire pattern of the forest economy in that area has been changed. For example, drift floating of timber on all the rivers draining into Baikal has been banned. Also, all sunken timber has been removed from the bottom of Baikal's tributaries.

Many more similar measures have been taken, but these are only the first steps. Soviet authorities are considering further steps to stimulate economic progress in the Baikal area without causing damage to its natural environment. For this purpose, the Academy of Sciences of the USSR, and other scientific organizations have launched an extensive research program involving the assessment of the present hydrochemical balance of the Baikal basin and its possible changes, given different variants of economic development in the area, as well as estimates of the impact such changes could exert on the local flora and fauna.

The results of such investigations make it possible to systematically verify the sufficiency and adequacy of the measures taken and to plan further progress of the local economy on a scientific basis.

Of course, we cannot as yet extend the whole complex of such measures to all the lakes and rivers of the country. However, Soviet scientists and economists believe that the measures taken to improve the situation in Lake Baikal, which have no parallel anywhere else in the world, not only will make it possible to establish rational interaction between the economy and the natural environment in this area but also will furnish practical experience and know-how in planning large-scale economic development projects so as to avoid serious environmental hazards.

Important measures are being taken to prevent atmospheric pollution. So far they have been limited to measures to improve the effectiveness of purifying installations whose use on a wide scale will considerably reduce (in spite of the rapid development of industrial production) the amounts of dust, carbon monoxide and some other pollutants discharged into the atmosphere.

In the fight to lower the high concentrations of atmospheric pollution, Soviet authorities take other measures as well, such as the reduction of discharge of industrial waste on days when the wind is not strong enough to disperse it. At present, more than 100 major industrial centers have a monitoring service to detect and warn factories about high levels of concentration of industrial waste in the atmosphere, and to have them reduce the amounts of discharge if the atmospheric conditions make it imperative.

Such warnings enable factories to considerably reduce the amounts of pollutants discharged, without slowing down production. In some cases, when meteorological conditions were particularly unfavorable, the discharge of pollutants dropped severalfold below the maximum permissible concentration levels.

Significantly, the purification systems now in use throughout the world are largely inadequate. It is necessary to change over from the so-called direct water supply in industry to the closed cycle, so that water would circulate uninterruptedly the same way as it does in the radiator of an automobile.

This is the best and most promising way of saving the water used in industry. In the Soviet Union, the amount of water in closed-circuit circulation back in 1966 was estimated at 65 cu km a year. By 1970 this figure had gone up to 98 cu km, which accounted for about 50 percent of the total amount of pure water saved. The expenditure of fresh water on industrial needs in 1980 remains the same as it was in 1975.

The key to solving the problem of clean air lies, according to specialists, in totally eliminating any discharge into the atmosphere. In heating systems, this has been achieved by burning natural gas. In Moscow the utilization of this smokeless fuel in its centralized heating system has made the air in this big industrial center virtually clean.

We are trying to use technical innovations for still more effective and rational utilization of resources, for preventing pollution of the natural environment and for its amelioration.

Of special importance are the growing possibilities for changing the structure and balance of renewable resources. Take, for example, changing the structure of water resources. The first attempts to modify the hydrographic network of rivers and lakes, for the purpose of building convenient transport routes and irrigation systems, were made in very early times. The building of dams, reservoirs and canals substantially modified the runoff and in this way made it possible to utilize the water in rivers more effectively. At present about 3 percent of the agricultural territory of the globe is irrigated. This means that a small fraction of the world's river flow is used in artificial irrigation.

Work on the transformation of natural resources for the purpose of making better use of them is being done to a varying extent in all countries. For the Soviet Union and the other socialist countries, such changes are regarded as an integral part of the comprehensive and unified national plans for economic development and for optimal use of natural resources. Many of the measures being taken are truly unique; no wonder they are carefully examined and discussed. For example, there was a long and heated argument among scientists over a project involving the construction of a hydropower station in the lower reaches of the Ob River. The water reservoir formed by its high dam would flood a vast area that is not used for farming in any way but is rich in oil and natural gas. So, after all the pros and cons had been weighed, the project was scrapped.

Another sweeping project under discussion involves the diversion of a part of the flow of large northern rivers in the European part of the USSR and Siberia in a southerly direction. This project raised a great many collateral economic physicogeographic problems, and now scientists and engineers are looking for the best ways of solving them.

Very promising experiments on breeding some varieties of fish in large lakes and seas have been carried out by Soviet scientists and fish-farming organizations. Thus the famous trout from Lake Sevan in the Caucasus have now found a second home in the giant Lake Issyk-Kul in Soviet Central Asia where they are bred for commercial fishing. The mullet of the Black Sea now live in the Caspian Sea. Before the fish were resettled in the new habitat, fish breeders had stocked the Caspian with feed from the Black Sea. Measures have been taken to improve the fisheries in the Sea of Azov and to set up special seal-breeding farms in the Caspian Sea.

The scope for rational utilization and management of natural resources is increasing and has transcended the boundaries of a single country. The Soviet Union is linked up with European countries by oil pipelines and electric power transmission lines, thus enabling these countries to use electric power, natural gas and oil from the USSR.

Today, the Soviet Union and these countries make optimal use of natural resources, in line with their common interests and according to the money and effort each contributes to the exploitation of the resources. Although the press often tends to blur or simply negate the distinctions between the ways in which capitalist and socialist economies interact with the natural environment, some Western scientists give due consideration to these distinctions. Pointing up the similarity in the *technical aspect* of prevention of environmental pollution in the USA and the USSR, Prof. Barry Commoner writes in his book *The Closing Circle:*

> In response to these difficulties, a strong ecological movement seems to be developing in the USSR; members of the scientific community have criticized industrial developments that ignore or underemphasize environmental effects, and citizens, as everywhere, complain of the resulting pollution. Recent government actions appear to presage a more vigorous ecologically oriented control over industrial planning. Here, of course, the socialist system in the Soviet Union does have an important practical advantage over the private enterprise system. Nationwide, all-encompassing plans for industrial and agricultural development—indeed, for nearly every aspect of economic life—are an intrinsic feature of the Soviet system. The advantage of such planning in any effort to alleviate environmental problems hardly needs to be demonstrated to anyone familiar with the chaotic environmental situation in the United States— where AEC atomic safety regulations have been challenged by several states; where government officials are engaged in a long, frustrating battle with the auto industry over pollution standards; where the need for ecologically sound agriculture comes in conflict with the economic interests of the producers of fertilizers and synthetic pesticides.
>
> Finally, the socialist system may have an advantage over the private enterprise system, with respect to the basic relationship between economic processes and ecological imperatives. (26, p. 280)

Why does the Soviet press carry so many articles criticizing industrial managers at plants and factories that pollute the environment, and why is so much attention given to disturbing situations in areas adversely affected by industry?

Do we really think that in the Soviet Union the optimal relationship between society and the natural environment has been achieved? No, we don't, and Soviet people are well aware of the reasons why.

The rich and varied natural resources of our country, and the vastness of its territory, and the comparatively low density of population have over the centuries fostered a care-free attitude to the natural environment. The abovementioned measures to organize nature preserves and to conserve natural resources, taken during the first two decades after the 1917 socialist revolution, were a matter of principle and were not prompted by the fear that a disruption of the ecological balance might be harmful to the people's health or damaging to the nation's economy, for in those days no such disruption was yet in sight.

While recovering from the severe damage inflicted by the foreign military intervention and the civil war in 1918-1919; while building our industry in the 1930s, which put a tremendous strain on the nation's resources and manpower; and later, while rehabilitating the ravaged economy after the nazi invasion in World War II, the Soviet government was unable to allocate sufficiently large sums of money for these purposes. But even then the Soviet state did all it could to protect the natural environment and the health of the country's population.

The Soviet Union was the first country to establish limits for permissible concentration levels of pollutants in water and air. Significantly, these are the most stringent limits that have so far been imposed anywhere in the world, for they allow of concentrations that are the least harmful to human health. The government has also adopted many laws, which we mentioned earlier in this account.

A fundamental change in the attitude to nature occurred in the late 1960 and the early 1970s. In the first place, the development of industry, the industrialization of agriculture and land improvement had reached such levels that people's intrusion upon nature was finally showing certain negative effects. Second, we studied the experience of the United States, FRG, Japan and some other industrially advanced countries where the environmental situation had grown very serious indeed. Very important measures were taken by the Supreme Soviet of the USSR at its session specially called for this purpose in September 1972, following a lengthy discussion on various environmental problems.

The fact that so much attention is devoted to these questions, in a country where the level of environmental pollution is at least 1/20 that in the United States, in the FRG and in other technically advanced countries, gives us confidence that the Soviet Union will cope with this problem successfully.

What is actually being done to fight environmental pollution?

The Soviet hydrometeorological service, which has stations and outposts strategically located all over the country, monitors environmental conditions and reports the incidence of pollutants in the air, water and soil. In addition to this, the sanitary-epidemiological service of the Ministry of Public Health, special inspection teams of the Ministry for Land Improvement and the Water Economy, and the Ministry for Fisheries monitor the incidence of toxic substances. Special organizations keep an eye on the operation of water- and air-purification installations at factories and plants. None of these organizations, it should be noted, is subordinate to the ministry responsible for the particular industry involved.

Each ministry is required to observe the laws and decisions of the government with regard to the natural environment and its resources, but in addition to all the Soviet governmental bodies, there are also special organizations that enforce these laws. For example, the USSR State Forestry Committee keeps an eye on the condition of the forests and their restoration, while the cutting of timber and its use is the job of the Ministry of Timber and Woodworking Industry and organizations directly concerned with it. The observance of the correct and effective exploitation of mineral deposits is the responsibility of the State Committee for the Inspection of Mines.

Measures for the protection of the environment and for the rational utilization of its resources have, since 1975, formed an important section of the state plan for the development of the national economy that is adopted by the Supreme Soviet of the USSR each year.

The brevity of the sessions of the Supreme Soviet may create the false impression that it does not devote enough time to discussing important matters (which is often mentioned in the American and West-European press). This is not true. Both chambers of the Supreme Soviet of the USSR have a large number of standing commissions concerned with the fundamental economic problems of this country (commissions for industry, trade, agriculture, for the affairs of the youth, etc.). All these commissions are made up of deputies whose knowledge, experience and interests are best suited for the job. More than 30 percent of the members of the Supreme Soviet are at the same time members of these commissions. There are also commissions for environmental protection.

Before the reports on the execution of the state plan and budget for the current year, and the guidelines for the economic plan and budget for the next year are submitted to the Supreme Soviet for discussion, they are given thorough scrutiny by its commissions.

Thus the Commission for Nature Conservation, of which the author is a member, hears reports from eight-ten ministries whose factories pollute the natural environment. The ministers involved sometimes have to listen to sharply critical remarks and take into account proposals to readjust their plans. The commission also studies reports from supervising bodies and submits its recommendations to the Supreme Soviet. Some of these recommendations are incorporated in current plans and others, of a more fundamental character, are used in drawing up guidelines for future planning.

At its 25th Congress, the Communist Party of the Soviet Union devoted special attention to the problem of environmental protection. In his speech at that Congress, Alexei Kosygin, Chairman of the Council of Ministers of the USSR, reported on guidelines for the development of the national economy of the USSR for the 1976-1980 period. He said:

> The scale of economic activity in the Tenth Five-Year Plan period and the specifics of the modern technological processes used in industry, particularly in branches such as metallurgy and the chemical industry, require special measures to *protect the environment.* Large allocations are envisaged in most industries for these purposes. New methods and means of controlling the ejection of noxious

waste into the atmosphere are to be used, and provision is being made for the comprehensive and rational use and protection of water and forest resources. All industries are to be switched to the utilization of recycled water. For instance, in the chemical industry, despite considerable growth in production, the discharge of industrial effluent into rivers and lakes and the ejection of noxious wastes into the atmosphere will be reduced, while the utilization of fresh water for industrial purposes in 1980 will remain at the 1975 level. (8, p. 152)

Western journalists write that in the USSR a factory manager who breaks the rules regulating the work of industry vis-à-vis the natural environment pays but a very small fine compared to the bonus he gets for fulfilling the plan. In fact, he breaks these rules, they say, precisely because he is required to meet the targets of his production plan.

Such violations did take place, it is true, but all that is a thing of the past. Now the situation has changed drastically. Industrial managers who have allowed large quantities of industrial waste to be discharged into the atmosphere or into a river can be prosecuted on criminal charges. The Soviet press carries a large number of reports of this kind.

On February 4, 1975, the newspaper *Pravda* carried an editorial which examined the Decision of the Central Committee of the CPSU and the Council of Ministers of the USSR "On Measures to Prevent the Pollution of the Basin of the Sea of Azov and the Black Sea".

The decision noted that as the result of the operation of waste-treatment facilities and water conservation schemes at factories, cities and health resorts around the Black Sea and the Sea of Asov, and of other measures taken to this effect, the amount of untreated effluent and other industrial wastes discharged into these basins has been reduced considerably.

At the same time, the decision called attention to the inadequate capacity of some waste-treatment facilities in view of the growing volume of housing and industrial construction. The document pointed out that the ministries responsible for the work of some factories had not acted promptly enough to adopt advanced techniques to prevent environmental pollution, to solve the problem of multiple processing of raw material and utilization of waste.

The Central Committee of the CPSU and the Council of Ministers of the USSR directed the governments of the Russian Federation, the Ukraine, Byelorussia and Georgia, and the executive bodies of the relevant industries to enforce the measures listed in the decision, in order to completely eliminate the discharge of industrial and domestic effluent before the end of 1984. In some cities, and at a number of factories, the discharge of effluent was discontinued by 1980. All ships sailing the seas and the rivers that flow into them must be equipped with mechanisms for collecting waste and delivering it ashore. Collective farms and state farms were directed to see to it that no poisonous chemicals would get into rivers. The USSR Ministry for Land Improvement was directed to act jointly with the governments of the Russian Federation, the Ukraine and Georgia in drawing up a regional scheme of nature conservation and the rational use of the natural resources of the Black Sea and the Sea of Azov for the period ending in 2000.

Rational utilization of natural resources and a thrifty attitude to the environment were the subject of an *Izvestia* editorial entitled "Nature and Man", published on February 11, 1976. Besides giving an overall analysis of this problem in the USSR, the article contained a number of suggestions from *Izvestia* readers (most of which had been published in that newspaper) with regard to the proposed guidelines for the 10th five-year plan of economic development.

It must be noted here that state supervisory organizations have enlisted the services of hundreds of thousands of volunteer assistants, members of the societies for the protection of the natural environment in all the constituent Soviet republics, also members of the Geographic Society and many other societies, clubs and movements, such as societies of young naturalists, societies of young Michurinites (named after the Soviet scientist Ivan Michurin).

The staff members of research organizations and individual scientists take an important part in the protection of the natural environment. There are many scientific councils all over the country which cooperate in studying different aspects of this problem. In their articles and in their speeches, scientists make critical remarks and offer numerous suggestions aimed at improving the environmental situation. For example, the Soviet press has carried numerous articles about the expediency of charging money for the use of water, land and other natural resources that are the property of the entire people.

The Soviet economic system incorporates the use of various means for combating the deterioration of the environment. At present, we are improving the rules and standards regulating the utilization of natural wealth. Some economists consider it expedient to introduce economic incentives in the form of bonuses to be paid when there is some economy of a given resource. (In all cases, naturally, it is always government organizations that will settle such accounts.) Each of these proposals and suggestions has its positive and negative aspects. The discussion is still going on.

To conclude this chapter, I would like to add that public ownership of natural resources and the means of production, which constitute the basis of the socialist system, and the planned character of the development of socialist society, offer every opportunity for the building of an optimal system of relationships between human beings and nature, as the experience of the Soviet Union and the other socialist states has shown.

However, as we have repeatedly stressed for all the vastness of the Soviet Union's territory, and, in fact, the territory of all the socialist countries taken together, it would not be possible for them to resolve this problem in its entirety, precisely because nature conservation is a global problem.

How and when the environmental problem will be solved depends on two key factors. First, scientific and technological progress will enable us to pass from describing nature to shaping it. The second factor is social progress which, in the words of Karl Marx, is the only thing capable of ensuring the transition from a spontaneously developing culture to a culture people can direct consciously for their own good.

CHAPTER THREE

FROM SPONTANEOUSLY DEVELOPING TO CONSCIOUSLY DIRECTED CIVILIZATION

HUMANS SHAPE NATURE

At its every stage society's interaction with the natural environment puts a new angle on our requirements for information about the natural environment, and on the development of the earth sciences.

On the one hand, these sciences have arisen out of the long experience of man's interaction with nature. On the other hand, the earth sciences serve as a means to further expand this interaction and make it more effective.

The earth sciences furnish fresh information about the natural environment and its resources and in this way help human beings to protect themselves from adverse elemental phenomena, and to find more natural wealth and to put it to work. This aim continues to exist today.

But there is still another task that is growing in importance: to create techniques for predicting how natural conditions will change under the impact of human activity, whether deliberate or unintentional. This is a very difficult task, and many specialists doubt that it is feasible at all. Therefore some of them demand that all anthropogenic modification of the environment be stopped, since nobody can say for certain what these changes may lead to. However, the influence of man upon nature, and the transformation of nature are inevitable. People's influence on the natural environment has become worldwide, and its intensity is growing all the time and will continue to do so in the future.

Research on some natural features has over the entire period of man's existence been connected with the work to adapt these features for his own use. For example, the hydrology of inland waters, pedology [soil science] and forest science have been growing side by side with hydraulic engineering, agronomy and forestry.

However, until recently the scale of such transformations—the portion of a natural resource being transformed, and people's impact on the long established natural processes—has been insignificant.

Now all this has changed dramatically.

Today, giant power, land-improvement and transport hydrotechnical projects can, in a very short time, change river systems to a much greater degree than the natural fluviomorphological processes have done over thousands of years. Reconstructed river systems constitute a sizeable proportion of the entire river network of the globe. Still more marked are changes being made in the condition of the soil, forests, and other elements of the biosphere.

The present-day level of technology and know-how ensures rapid development of such projects and schemes. But we are still unable to properly assess our own capability to calculate and predict all the consequences and implications of man's interference with the structure and composition of the natural environment.

It is fairly easy to calculate the amount of time it takes to create a water reservoir, but it is far more difficult to predict its future biochemical status and its fishing possibilities, the washout of its shores and the effect of a sudden rise of subsoil waters.

It is easy to exterminate all agricultural pests (and together with them all the other insects, as is often the case) over a large area, but it is difficult to foresee what new ecological balance may develop in that area and when, or what ultimate effect such a balance might have on the crop we have tried to protect.

It is easy to explode a nuclear device at an altitude of 100-200 kilometers, but it is still unclear just what perturbations may occur in the sensitive upper atmospheric layers as the result of such an explosion.

Thus, the tasks we mentioned above are the focus of attention by earth scientists. They are numerous and complicated, particularly because there already exist means by which people can regulate natural processes, and because there are unstable conditions in the environment that make it possible for people to interfere with elemental processes with relative ease.

Let us take a look at the present state of the earth sciences and the prospects for their development in the light of the problems under review.

Information about the condition of the phenomena under study is of tremendous importance for all earth sciences. Research in every field of knowledge begins with the information that the researcher has at his disposal. However, unlike the sciences which have long since used experimentation as their basis for obtaining data in a particular field of research, ecology is a sphere where scientists have to process tremendous amounts of information to find the few facts and data they need. The more comprehensive is the character of the phenomenon under study, the more information they have to analyze.

It is not accidental that due to the very logic of the development of sciences about the earth, the systems of obtaining and processing information are being re-equipped fundamentally.

The most important aspects of the developing technology of observation are the use of telemetric systems, mobile platforms and various remote-control methods.

A few decades ago, all measurements—of temperature, of intensity of the magnetic field, of speeds of currents in rivers and seas, and of other characteristics of the environment—were taken, as in the century or two preceding, only at the point of observation.

In 1930, the Soviet Union launched the first radiometer probe which also was probably the world's first telemetry system. After that, the first automatic meteorological stations were set up in remote locations on the land surface of the USSR and on drifting ice floes in the Arctic. Alongside these stations which transmitted data on weather conditions at regular intervals, Soviet weathermen also launched special meteorological rockets in the 1950s. At present, telemetry systems are used for various meteorological, oceanographic and other geophysical measurements. They have assumed special importance in space research, where a complex system of measurement instruments and facilities mounted in spacecraft is sent out to collect information from other celestial bodies hundreds of millions of kilometers away from the earth.

During the past several decades, wide use has been made of airplanes specially equipped to quickly determine the condition of the atmosphere and various characteristics of the earth's surface over large areas, by means of magnetic observation survey, by mapping large ice floes in the seas and by measuring the temperature of seawater. The survey techniques were vastly improved with the launching of special space probes that circle the earth and flash back much of the vital information about our planet.

The utilization of space probes has created essentially new capabilities for obtaining information about various processes taking place on earth. Significantly, space probes came to the aid of scientists at the time when their need for a wider spectrum and volume of information was very great.

The first thing they did with the help of man-made satellites was to obtain atmospheric data. Never before could meteorologists hope to see the atmosphere over the whole of the globe, or be able to observe the formation and movement of clouds, the zones of precipitation and many other phenomena.

Thousands, even tens of thousands, of observers on all continents could now see the atmosphere and collect vital information, which was then disseminated via a ramified system. At present four or five weather satellites, those in geostationary orbit and those on polar orbits do a good deal of this work, and are expected to do almost all of it in the future.

The information that scientists obtain from the satellites is becoming increasingly varied and exhaustive, including the quantity and even the quality of the ice in the seas and oceans, the location of ice fields, the accumulation of snow in the mountains, the condition of forests and agricultural crops, and even the geological structure of the earth's crust.

The recording by satellites of infrared radiation and high radio-frequency range radiation that emanates from the surface of the earth, from clouds and from different layers of the atmosphere enables scientists to measure the temperature of the surface of the land or the sea, to establish temperature patterns in the atmosphere according to altitudes, to observe the quantity of vegetation in the fields, the state of crops and forests, the location of polluted areas on the surface of the seas and oceans, the movement of schools of fish, and many other elements of the environment.

So far, the natural radiation emanating from the earth's surface has been used in circumterrestrial survey only as a passive source of information. Still broader possibilities for obtaining information will be opened up with the help of active probing from satellites using radar, laser beams, etc. But these possibilities will be available only after more powerful energy generating sources have been developed, specially for use in satellites.

The use of satellites has stimulated the development of new techniques for probing the lithosphere, the hydrosphere and the atmosphere by remote control. For a long time, geophysicists used the passage of natural seismic waves through our planet and the spread of acoustic waves from powerful explosions in the air for studying the inner structure of the earth and its atmosphere. This led to the use of artificially induced seismic, acoustic and hydroacoustic waves for studying the structure of the earth's crust, the atmosphere and the ocean. The study in the radio-frequency range has proved very effective for discovering and measuring the characteristics of many atmospheric phenomena, such as ionization in the upper layers of the atmosphere, and the precipitation, formation of clouds and some other phenomena that take place in its lower regions.

The use of telemetric methods and mobile measurement systems calls for automation of analysis and its processing, because of the high speed at which data is obtained and the tremendous amount of information to be processed. All these operations are now fully computerized.

Observation of the earth's surface, using sophisticated recording equipment and data-processing techniques, are widely used by meteorological services. At present automatic lines have been established to cover the full cycle of operations—from obtaining and analyzing meteorological and hydrological information and data, flashed by earth-based stations or orbiting satellites, down to the drawing up of maps which then go to the weatherman's desk.

The need to have global information about all the media of our planet necessitates the development of international co-operation, in order to coordinate methods of observation, promptly collect data and pass it on to different countries for circulation there.

Such cooperation in the field of meteorology has been developing for a long time. The World Meteorological Organization has existed for more than a hundred years. The world weather watch, which at present integrates the activities of weathermen throughout the world, is a complex network system which can promptly collect and disseminate weather information among all of its members over a whole hemisphere in 3-5 hours, and over the whole of our planet in 6-8 hours.

Similar international organizations were later set up to exchange information on the phenomena of terrestrial magnetism, on earthquakes, on the condition of the world ocean, etc.

Also successful are the efforts of geologists in different countries to coordinate the results of their research. During the past ten years of cooperation, hydrologists in many countries have obtained reliable information about moisture circulation and about the water balance of our planet.

We receive information about the planetary processes taking place in inorganic nature—in the lithosphere, hydrosphere, and atmosphere. Although the volume of information and the speed at which it is processed still fall short of geophysicists' expectations, the rapid development of technology gives us every reason to assert that in the near future the shortcomings in this field will be eliminated.

It is much more difficult to ensure a steady flow of information about the vital functions of the biota—i.e., the entire aggregate of living organisms on our planet.

It is necessary to examine the reaction of the biota to anthropogenic changes in the biosphere, but it is utterly impossible systematically to observe the condition of all the plant and animal species on earth. What criteria should be used to assess the state of the biota? Where should such observation outposts be set up? And what condition should be regarded as "normal"? At present, national research centers and various international organizations are discussing the expediency of setting up a system of local and worldwide monitoring services to keep the condition of the biosphere—i.e., the state of the biota—under day-to-day observation.

There is no doubt that all these questions will be solved, and that a monitoring system which will provide a steady flow of information about the condition of the biota (and, consequently, the whole of the biosphere) will be set up in the near future.

A new fundamental feature of earth sciences today is research on phenomena taking place on a global and even a cosmic scale.

Both in the interests of basic research and for more immediate practical purposes, scientists are increasingly drawn to the study of phenomena related to the whole of our planet. This is also prompted by the growing importance of the "global" elements in our practical work. Communication channels and airline routes are getting longer, and the development of submarine deposits of mineral wealth is moving farther and farther away from shore. Pollution and other modifications of the natural environment that take place in one country have effects far outside its territorial limits. Perturbations in the atmosphere caused by nuclear explosions and the launching of space ships have a global effect. And finally, space flights and human activities in the near regions of outer space also have a global character.

In this connection, all information about the state of the natural environment on the whole of our planet, as well as our understanding of the processes unfolding over all of it, become increasingly important, in purely practical terms. Problems directly related to outer space are also becoming increasingly important.

The geochemist studying the circulation of substances on earth naturally wants to know more about the general laws which govern the circulation of substances on the other planets of the solar system in different periods of their existence.

The meteorologist is concerned with the study of not only the atmosphere of the earth but also the atmospheres of other celestial bodies. Man's ambition to land on other planets has put a practical angle on their ideas about the structure and properties of their atmospheres. Thus, some of the parameters have already been established for the atmosphere and the surface of the planet Mars. The successful landing and long operation of Soviet automatic stations on the surface of Venus in 1975 were made possible by earlier probing and research on the properties of that planet's atmosphere. Scientists concerned with other geophysical phenomena are interested in similar problems.

This aspect of development of the earth sciences exemplifies the current "cosmocization" of science. At the same time it facilitates our understanding of the possibilities of changes of the environment on a global scale.

Significantly, the research programs range over all aspects of complex phenomena taking place on the borderlines of the different "spheres" of our planet, and affecting these spheres.

This leads, just as in other sciences, to the merging of what used to be different disciplines, and to the emergence of new marginal disciplines.

Right from the first decades of our century, the few disciplines of a more or less general character such as astronomy, geography, geology, botany, zoology and others, gave rise to a multitude of specialized, clearly delineated fields of research: meteorology, hydrology of the waters of the land, oceanology, astrophysics, etc. At present, roughly since the 1950s, alongside further ramification, the process has been reversed to a certain extent, and scientists specializing in one area are more and more inclined to study phenomena and solve problems by drawing on the experience and methods used in other fields. Only in this way can the close links between all the elements of our planet be revealed and understood. The atmosphere and the ocean; the atmosphere, the ocean and the earth's shell; geophysical phenomena and the biota (the aggregate of living organisms) are interconnected.

Even such seemingly unrelated sciences as geophysics and biology are beginning to converge.

The attention that biologists devote to the populations of certain organisms, or to the study of whole complexes of such populations which form biocenoses, leads naturally to an interest in the connections between individual organisms, populations and the environment, known as biogeocenosis. This term refers to the stable aggregate of populations of various organisms in certain conditions and within the framework of the inorganic natural environment.

It is the job of ecology as a science to study in their entirety the interconnections between living organisms and the environment. And this opens up a new area of knowledge, covering a wide spectrum of phenomena and methods of research.

The countless interwoven processes that link an organism with its organic and inorganic habitat highly complicate this job. But, at the same time, ecology as a science is called upon to evaluate (on the basis of a complex analysis of information drawn from various disciplines) the effects of the unintentional anthropogenic impact on the environment, and the deliberate action aimed at modifying it.

The basic and more difficult elements of such estimates are the calculation and prognostication of future episodes in the natural environment which may be expected in the course of natural processes taking place, and also as the results of unintentional and deliberate action by human beings. This calculation may be based on a statistical analysis of information about similar events in the past. However, calculations allow for the emergence of certain meanings of the sought quantity over certain lengthy periods in the future.

After long and careful meteorological observations from a given place on earth, it may very well be possible to evaluate the average and the lowest temperatures of the air in January for many years to come. The processing of seismic observations would make it possible to draw up a map of seismic activity, indicating the probability or earthquakes of a given range of intensity, in any region, for several decades. An analysis of ships' logs makes it possible to outline a pattern of distribution of schools of cod in the Barents Sea during the fishing season, etc.

Such assessments are taken into consideration in the designing of hydropower stations, residential houses and other structures, and in long-term planning of various kinds, such as estimating winter fuel reserves for a city in a given part of the country.

Statistical calculations can be made even without a theoretical analysis of the process in question, so long as one is sure that it had the same character in the past (accumulation of the information used), and the future, when the events thus calculated are expected to occur.

Statistical calculations are not reliable when we must consider changes in the character of the processes under review, such as a changing climate. Incidentally, as is well known, the climate can change somewhat over a period of 100-200 years.

Much more reliable are calculations based on the quantitative theory of this process, on our knowledge of the functional connection of the quantity in question with the initial data, on the completeness of the initial data and the known quantities of the parameters characterizing these connections. Such are all the basic technical and engineering calculations.

The state of the earth sciences today enables us to use such calculations in the assessment of future events in but very few cases. A good example is the calculation of the ocean tide at various points of the coast, or the calculation of the highest level of spring floods in the lower reaches of a river, knowing the amount of rainfall in that river's catchment area.

In a large number of cases, we can use only the qualitative or incomplete quantitative theory of this process, and only a fraction of the facts that we need to achieve a high degree of accuracy of our calculation.

However, our everyday activities call for the assessment of the future state of many elements of the biosphere.

One type of assessment is forecasting. There is a wide variety of methods whereby events in the biosphere (weather, condition of the ionosphere, ice-drift on a river, storms at sea, a propagation of agricultural pests, etc.) can be forecast.

In most cases, forecasts are based on an analysis (mostly qualitative) of trends in the process in question. They may include some numerical calculations, too. Moreover, extensive use is made of comparison of the situation being analyzed with similar situations observed in the past. Such, in essence, are common synoptical methods of weather forecasting. Similar methods are used for prognosticating events taking place in the ionosphere and the magnetosphere, the state of agricultural crops, and many other phenomena.

Forecasting, as a rule, provides highly accurate quantitative characteristics of a given phenomenon, such as the temperature of the air for the next day, but, unlike calculations—whether statistical or those based on functional associations—forecasts may prove to be incorrect. Every method of prognostication has a margin of probability, but we can never be certain that our assessment will prove correct in each individual case.

Deviations from the "normal" condition of the processes taking place in the atmosphere and hydrosphere are in most cases primary, in relation to various phenomena occurring in the biosphere as a whole, and particularly in the biota.

When sharp anomalies occur, the mechanism of this influence is readily traceable. Thus, a deviation of the Kuroshio Current from its usual course caused large masses of fish to migrate to other parts of the ocean. And this led to changes in the character of commercial fishing in a vast area of the western part of the Pacific.

A similar situation occurs off the coast of Peru, where the El Niño Current, for reasons so far unknown, changes its course once in several decades which causes not only the migration of masses of fish but also certain meteorological phenomena that may have an ill effect for the economy of the coastal regions of that country.

That even large populations of certain animals and plants can die out because of drought, cold winter or excessive snowfall is well known.

Therefore, the forecasting of geophysical conditions, and, more specifically, weather forecasting, is seen to be the leading and, in fact, the primary element of a wider problem—the forecasting of the condition of all the main elements of the biosphere.

With all the imperfections of the weather forecasting service, we can "tell the weather" with a much higher degree of accuracy than we do other phenomena taking place in the biosphere. There is nothing surprising about the fact that meteorologists were among the first to adopt qualitative analysis which replaced statistics and which helped them develop quantitative theories, based on the achievements of physics and mathematics.

The transition from the essentially descriptive methods of weather forecasting to its physico-mathematical analysis is typical of all earth sciences. It has been induced not only by the universal logic of development of any sphere of knowledge (as is known, all scientific disciplines now have, to a varying degree, been put on a mathematical footing), but also by the sharply increased requirements for accurate information about the state of the natural environment.

In the building industry, faulty calculations of environmental parameters may lead to safety factors that are either insufficient or excessive, the latter involving unjustifiably great expenses. With the growing scale of construction, such financial losses might be very great indeed.

The same applies to the forecasting of future conditions of the environment, which are important for planning various economic projects.

To develop objective methods of calculating and forecasting future environmental conditions—which is the most difficult problem facing all earth sciences—will become possible only if these methods have a solid physico-mathematical basis.

We are steadily moving toward methods of calculating future atmospheric processes—toward more precise forecasting. Modern methods of weather forecasting for a period ranging from several hours to three days, make it possible to calculate certain important elements of the future situation in the atmosphere, such as the field of pressure, the field of wind, and the field of vertical air currents. The weatherman's job is to deduce the imminent weather conditions and provide such vital facts as the amount and time of precipitation, the character of cloudiness. To do so, he uses mainly qualitative methods of forecasting.

There are many unresolved difficulties still holding back our efforts to develop reliable methods of calculating and forecasting weather and other natural phenomena, but the volume of research carried out on this problem in many countries is growing and its results are good.

Weather forecasting is becoming more and more accurate (although not as rapidly as we would like to see it), largely owing to a recent proliferation of methods. But it has now become possible to create methods of long-term meteorological forecasting based on reliable calculations.

With the growing need for information about the natural environment, new types of prognostications of environmental conditions are being developed, and relevant services are being set up. For example, the ionosphere monitoring service has been operating in many countries for close to thirty years. The Soviet Union and the United States have services set up to monitor the radiation situation in outer space. Seismologists have gone a long way in developing reliable methods of forecasting earth tremors.

Forecasting as a method is also used in biology. For example, scientists have learned how to prognosticate the condition of farm crops and the size of the harvest to be taken in. They can also tell in advance the time agricultural pests will appear and the routes of fish migrations in the ocean.

All these facts inspire confidence that science will cope with the task of developing reliable methods of forecasting various phenomena taking place in the natural environment.

A still more formidable task facing scientists is how to develop methods of calculating the modification of natural conditions which result from unintentional and/or deliberate anthropogenic action on the environment.

The most alarming unintentional impact of man's activities is environmental pollution, and we shall now discuss the problem of calculating the effects of such pollution.

Today we can no longer say that the environment is polluted from just one source and that as the result of the natural "self-purification" processes it can easily recover its natural purity.

The basins of the big rivers that flow through densely populated industrial areas (i. e., almost all the rivers in the United States, Japan, in European countries, including two-thirds of all the rivers in the European part of the USSR) have long since ceased to be in what we used to call a "natural state". They have been turned into transport arteries, sources of electric power, water supply and, at the same time, sewage-disposal systems.

At present, these rivers account for about 20 percent of the fluvial runoff in the world. In the next century, almost all the rivers in the world will be used this way. The same can be said about the air in and around large industrial centers.

Permissible concentrations of pollutants flushed into rivers or discharged into the atmosphere are deduced by evaluating the limits of such concentrations considered safe for people, animals and plants.

We must not ignore the fact that more and more new elements go into the waste material, so that medical experts and biologists cannot keep pace and calculate relevant permissible concentrations for all of them. Besides, permissible-level calculations are based on the assessment of the direct action of a given element on the organism of a human being or an animal, while in actual fact people and animals are exposed to many elements, which act simultaneously and enter into chemical reactions and form new substances. This is precisely the situation that is taking shape in and around large industrial centers and indeed in whole countries that have high concentrations of industry and population.

The calculation of permissible discharges is rather primitive: the discharge must not create concentrations above permissible levels in the atmosphere of a given environment. However, it is easy to understand that differences in river systems or in atmospheric conditions (the speed of the current or the wind, the peculiarities of intermixture of water currents or air currents, etc.) have a marked effect on the transference and dissemination of all the waste discharged.

Meteorological and hydrological processes transfer, disseminate and, usually, disperse industrial wastes. In contrast, biological phenomena stimulate their selective accumulation and concentration. While passing through food chains, some of the elements finally find their way into the human organism in concentrations thousands of times higher than the concentration of the same substances found on the surface of the land, in the water or in the air.

In each of the numerous processes of interaction of a given element with the environment, and later with a living organism, one should bear in mind the state of instability and the existence of possible chain reactions that might emerge, when the input effect loses its earlier (e. g. linear) dependence on the concentration of elements and changes sharply, with even the slightest rise in this concentration.

Earlier we mentioned actions leading to pollution and the assessment of their impact on an individual organism or the population. In many cases, however, this impact sets off a whole chain of ecological events in the biosphere.

Pollution-induced disease, leading to the reduction or even the destruction of the population of some animal or plant species will inevitably stimulate the propagation of another species which, for example, the animal species in question fed on, or, for some other reason, the size of the population of the predators that normally subsist on them will also shrink.

Finally, it is important to take into account the need to calculate the entire complex of environmental changes—all the "reactions" taking place in the regional and even global environment, all the changes that occur as the result of this intrusion into the structure of the environment—and to allow for all other existing forms of modification and for those that may develop in the future.

Will scientists be able to cope with this task? They must and they will. At present, the earlier, somewhat primitive assessments of the effect that environmental pollution caused by some substance has on one or two animal or plant species are giving way to analyses of the entire chain of reactions that occur in the environment as the result of the emergence of a new substance. Such analyses, carried out in very complicated and difficult situations, are given in the book *The Closing Circle* in which Barry Commoner describes, among other things, the origins and nature of the famous Los Angeles smog and the measures being taken to deal with it and similar environmental maladies.

The unexpectedness of the adverse effects that the spread of certain substances has on the natural environment must not in any way be considered due to the complexity of the scientific problems which have emerged but to the fact that these problems have for a long time not even been considered by researchers.

We shall now discuss some of the transformations of weather and climate which, on the one hand, just like environmental pollution, come from unintentional anthropogenic activity, and on the other, are the result of people's deliberate action. We shall concentrate on an important specific feature of meteorological processes, a feature which we mentioned earlier in this account; the intermittent instability of meteorological processes, and the consequent emergence of spontaneous reactions.

In practical terms, it is impossible to stop all undesirable meteorological and other natural processes, if only because they contain such colossal amounts of energy. In this respect the anthropogenic modifications of weather and climate show us how those processes should be regulated.

The atmosphere has no permanent channels of control. Consequently, we must try to find, in this maze of atmospheric processes, those intermittently operating chains of interconnected phenomena that we can use as channels of control.

Atmospheric phenomena take shape in the process ot close interaction and conflict of opposites. Any air mass retains its physical characteristics for a fairly long time. However, once it finds itself in certain conditions, it changes its physical properties very sharply. Thus, even a small drop in the percentage of water vapor in the air near the saturation point, can produce fog or clouds, which sharply change the optical characteristics of a part of the atmosphere, thus creating different conditions for heat exchange between the atmosphere and the soil, etc.

The atmosphere is also very sensitive to the presence of certain admixtures, even in quantities which are infinitesimally small compared to the mass of air containing them. For example, in addition to the necessary concentration of water vapor in the air, the cloud-formation process also requires the presence of so-called condensation nuclei, whose physical properties are responsible for the speed and character of cloud formation. But total mass of condensation nuclei necessary for the formation of a cloud system of a thousand cubic kilometers does not exceed one kilogram.

Meteorologists' main efforts at present are directed at stimulating or suppressing cloud formation and at inducing rainfall where necessary.

The most realistic way to modify a cloud is by stimulating crystallization of supercooled droplets of water in it. It takes but a small amount of stimulating agent—dry ice—which sharply cools the air and induces crystallization of drops—or some iodides, whose action is due to the similarity of their crystalline structure with that of ice. For example, it takes a mere 100-200 grams of dry ice, or a few grams of iodides, to crystallize one cubic kilometer of a supercooled cloud. This means that the principle of regulation operates here full force.

Intensified crystallization is used successfully to disperse low-lying clouds, prevent hail formation and induce additional precipitation. Clouds are seeded with the above-mentioned reagents (dry ice, silver iodide, etc.) with the aid of either an aeroplane, or special rockets or artillery shells.

The dispersion of supercooled clouds and fog has for several years been successfully used in some countries to opening up the weather over airports in winter.

With the dispersion of clouds, the energy which was earlier reflected from their upper sides into outer space, can now reach the earth and warm up the lower regions of the atmosphere, inducing certain changes in the natural meteorological processes. Experiments involving the dispersion of clouds over a territory of several thousand square kilometers, as carried out in the Soviet Union, did change the conditions of the lower layer of the atmosphere. As a result of these experiments, the additional amounts of heat energy which descended into the lower regions of the atmosphere over this territory reached 10^{14} calories. This amount is quite compatible with the energy involved in the processes occurring in the atmosphere over an area of up to a hundred thousand kilometers. In other words, we can now use the second trigger effect which, when used at the required time and in the required place, will enable us to generate atmospheric processes with a power greater by a factor of 10^2.

In practical terms, the application of artificial crystallization to prevent hailstorms is of special interest. A large team of Soviet scientists has been working on this problem, achieving notable results, with close to 5 million hectares now under hailstorm control. Significantly, these measures have reduced the amount of damage inflicted by hailstorms about 3-5 times. The Soviet method of hailstorm control has been adopted in other countries, too (Hungary, Yugoslavia, Bulgaria and Switzerland). Meteorologists in the United States have also started work on this problem.

Induced precipitation has come under scientific scrutiny all over the world. The crystallization of supercooled clouds leads to rain precipitation. However, using this method we can expect to draw only about 50 to 70 percent of the moisture contained in the clouds, while the clouds formed in the natural way yield about 10 to 20 times as much moisture as they contained at the moment of precipitation. This can be explained by the fact that for a certain time the clouds act as a kind of moisture generator, transforming the vapor in the air into liquid or crystalline moisture, which then precipitates upon the earth.

This "generator" draws its energy from the latent heat released by condensation or crystallization of moisture. As we mentioned before, a cloud can be formed only if a certain volume of vapor-laden air is raised to the cooler upper regions of the atmosphere. This ascent is made possible by a source of energy that is external to the given volume of air, such as the heat emanating from the warm surface of the earth, the upward movement of masses of air, etc. However, after the air masses, on reaching a certain altitude, have yielded up their vapors either by condensation or crystallization, the amount of energy thus released may prove quite sufficient for the further ascent of air masses, for the excitation of the upward moving currents, for drawing more masses of air into them, which in turn increases the energy of the initial process. Thus there emerges a self-sustaining reaction, in which clouds can grow without any "extraneous" energy sources. That is how powerful hailstorm and rainstorm clouds are formed.

Consequently, the problem of obtaining additional considerable amounts of precipitation boils down to our trying to make clouds operate precisely as such generators. At present, the ways of solving the problem are being outlined.

So far, clouds have been modified within a very narrow range of physical conditions. Nevertheless, experiments in modifying purely local features of weather serve as stepping-stones to artificially precipitating more violent natural processes, such as hurricanes.

American scientists have for some time been holding hurricane-moderation experiments, in which they are greatly aided by their long and painstaking research on the structure and physical characteristics of these formidable phenomena. Several of their aircraft, specially fitted for this purpose, have crisscrossed the entire hurricane system hundreds of times and at different levels. They have studied areas of storm formation that all other "normal" airliners give a wide berth to and avoid.

As the result of the hard work of both pilots and scientists, we now have valuable information about the nature of hurricanes. In some cases the scientists carried out operations to activate the crystallization of hurricane clouds. According to our American colleagues, the hurricane system must be further energized, i.e., additional amounts of energy must be injected into it (crystallization of drops, as we just said, yields up a considerable amount of energy). At the same time this additional amount of energy must be distributed more evenly, and in this way the most dangerous velocities of the raging wind can be reduced. So far, no definitive results of these experiments have been obtained, but scientists are quite confident they will eventually accomplish this challenging task.

Humanity's principal task in the future will be not modifying the climate but retaining it in its present form, making use of possible changes in the heat balance of the planet and redistribution of the sources of heat on its surface. Clearly, to succeed in both we must learn how to regulate the climate.

In our examination of the unintentional anthropogenic impact on the climate, we pointed out the climate's possible instability and, in this connection, its vulnerability to even a slight effect that humans might have on it. Consequently, episodes that set off spontaneous reactions are particularly dangerous when our influence on the environment is unintentional, but at the same time, holds a special place in our search for ways and means of consciouslly directed environmental modification.

The combination of hydrometeorological processes in the atmosphere and in the ocean can be likened to a heat-propelled machine. Since we can expect interruptions in its work due to its changing power and the changing distribution of the sources of heat and its emission from the engine, we could well expect some sort of compensatory action. It would hardly be realistic to condition the distribution of the main sources of anthropogenic heat, large industrial complexes or populated centers, on our ability to change the climate. However, if some day we have to set up sources of heat, such as thermonuclear power stations in the ocean, we shall probably have to consider such a possibility.

The heat balance can be changed in several ways in any region of the earth. One such way is regulation of cloud formation. Considering the fact that the clouds reflect about 70 percent of solar radiation, human beings can substantially increase or decrease the flow of heat entering the atmosphere in a given region or, in the same manner, to disperse or form clouds in the daytime; or, conversely, to create or disperse the cloud screen for the radiation of heat from the earth's surface at night. Above, we mentioned the possibility that such sporadic actions can affect the synoptical situation, and consequently, change the weather over a large area.

Another way to influence the thermal balance in a comparatively limited area is by changing the albedo—the reflective power of the earth's surface. This could be regulated by planting certain kinds of vegetation. The albedo can also be changed by irrigating or draining the earth's surface. Great changes in the reflective power of the earth are wrought by the first snowfall or by the melting away of the snow cover.

The alteration of the global heat balance caused by blocking solar radiation can be achieved by injecting considerable amounts of aerosols into the upper layers of the atmosphere.

According to Soviet and American scientists, an annual amount of one million tons of a suitable substance (e.g., sulfur, which would form microscopic droplets of sulfuric acid) in the atmosphere could markedly modify the earth's climate.

Difficult though it may be this operation is, nevertheless, quite feasible, provided many countries joined in it.

Interference in the dynamics of the atmosphere or the ocean would provide another means of modifying the climate. Mountain ranges, too, have a considerable effect on the climate not only of the adjoining areas, but also of outlying regions. We believe that specially designed structures, though not as formidable as the mountains themselves, could perform this role very well.

As we noted before, deviations of ocean currents from their normal course induce substantial changes in the weather. Control of such currents could be achieved by building the necessary hydrotechnical projects, thousands and thousands of times as big as those which we now build on rivers. In principle, there are no major obstacles that would make the construction of such high dams impossible.

It is well to recall the famous projects that were drawn up

J. Forrester studied only two aspects of the development of humankind, those he considers the most important: the depletion of natural resources and the growing pressure on the environment which neither nature, nor humans will long be able to endure.

D. Meadows and his co-authors also take up these problems as the most important of all.

> If the present growth trends in world population, industrialization, pollution, food production, and resource depletion continue unchanged, the limits to growth on this planet will be reached sometime within the next one hundred years. The most probable result will be a rather sudden and uncontrollable decline in both population and industrial capacity. (41, p. 23)

Later, however, they express their anxiety about the growing gap between the rich and poor countries.

> One of the most commonly accepted myths in our present society is the promise that a continuation of our present patterns of growth will lead to human equality. We have demonstrated in various parts of this book that present patterns of population and capital growth are actually increasing the gap between the rich and the poor on a worldwide basis, and that the ultimate result of a continued attempt to grow according to the present pattern will be a disastrous collapse. (41, pp. 178-179)

Dr. B. Commoner takes a similar stand on this problem:

> Everywhere in the world there is evidence of a deep-seated failure in the effort to use the competence, the wealth, the power at human disposal for the maximum good of human beings. (26, p. 294)

The authors of *The Limits to Growth*, just like Forrester, consider that a halt to progress, the transition to so-called "global equilibrium" may help humankind avoid the catastrophe it is heading for. They are convinced that mankind can achieve such an equilibrium.

> Man possesses, for a small moment in his history, the most powerful combination of knowledge, tools, and re-

sources the world has ever known. He has all that is phys-
ically necessary to create a totally new form of human
society—one that would be built to last for generations.
The two missing ingredients are a realistic, long-term
goal that can guide mankind to the equilibrium society
and the human will to achieve that goal. Without such a
goal and a commitment to it, short-term concerns will
generate the exponential growth that drives the world
system toward the limits of the earth and ultimate collapse. With that goal and that commitment, mankind would
be ready now to begin a controlled, orderly transition
from growth to global equilibrium. (41, pp. 183-184)

Global equilibrium, they say, means no change in the size of
population (i.e., equal number of births and deaths), constant
volume of industrial production, reduction to a minimum of all
the incoming and outgoing elements of the social balance, such
as the rates of birth and death, the investment of capital, and
the withdrawal of used-up equipment and old structures from
service.

They suggest that a special regulatory mechanism be developed
in order to prevent human society from upsetting this balance.
At the same time, they say, social balance does not at all mean
that society will never change. Any activity which requires no
major expenditure of nonrenewable resources and which does
not put too much pressure on the natural environment—education, the arts, religion, sport, basic science, etc.—can develop
freely.

Since the volume of material production is limited, any improvement in the methods of production will give members of
society more free time, which they can utilize for pursuing the
above mentioned activities and for improving the "quality" of
their life.

Such is the idyllic picture of the future which was drawn not
by a utopian dreamer but by people who claim that all their facts
and calculations are based on the implacable logic of the elec-
tronic computer.

The Meadows team was probably the last to insist that the
development of humankind should be halted, that the size of

population should be stabilized, that further industrialization should be discontinued (which would first of all badly hit the developing countries, since it would perpetuate the present low level of their development), that both production and consumption should be reduced.

In one of the reports to the Club of Rome *(Mankind at the Turning Point)* Mihajloo Mesarovic and Eduard Pestel thought it necessary that society should "limit its development", which they considered should be balanced out and coordinated on a world scale.

This is what they wrote:

> 1. The world can be viewed only *in reference to the prevailing differences in culture, tradition, and economic development,* i.e., as a system of interacting regions; a *homogeneous view of such a system is misleading.*
>
> 2. *Rather than collapse of the world system as such,* catastrophes or *collapses* on a regional level *could occur, possibly* long before the middle of the next *century, although in different regions for different reasons, and at different times. Since the world is a system, such catastrophes will be felt profoundly throughout the entire world.*
>
> 3. The solution to such catastrophes *of the world system* is possible only in the global context and by appropriate global actions. *If the framework for such joint action is not developed, none of the regions would be able to avoid the consequences. For each region, its turn would come in due time.*
>
> 4. *Such a global solution could be implemented only through* a balanced, differentiated growth *which is analogous to organic growth rather than* undifferentiated growth. *It is irrefutable that the second type of growth is* cancerous and would ultimately be fatal.
>
> 5. The delays in devising such global strategies *are not only detrimental or costly, but* deadly. *It is in this sense that we truly need* a strategy for survival. (42, p. 55)

Mesarovic and Pestel stress the need to close the gap between the standards of living of different social groups and in different regions of the world.

> Historically, evolution of any human society has been marked by the growth and decline of various gaps between different social groups. If a society is to preserve its integrity, widening of such gaps simply cannot persist; sooner or later the gaps will either be sufficiently narrowed or the fabric of the society will yield to centrifugal forces. Analogously, mankind cannot enter even the first stage of organic global growth if the economic gap between various world regions increases continuously; it is the question of survival of the world as such. (42, p. 57)

Alarmed by this state of affairs the authors offered to calculate the changing gaps between different social groups in the future.

> The results of the first scenario computer analysis (which corresponds to the historically established type of development—E.F.) are rather disquieting. Not only does the economic gap between rich and poor regions not narrow, but it increases considerably in terms of ratios and appallingly in absolute terms. The gap between the average per capita incomes in the Western industrialised countries grouped according to our classification in the Developed World Region ... and in Latin America (Region 6) will increase from 5 to 1 to almost 8 to 1 or, in absolute terms, from about $2,000 to more than $10,000 per capita. The situation in South Asia would be even worse. The per capita income gap between the Developed World and South Asia (Region 9) and similarly Tropical Africa (Region 8) would increase in absolute terms from nearly $2,500 to $13,000 while in relative terms the per capita income ratio will remain above 20 to 1. *If one relies on the prevailing economic patterns, trying to close this gap might as well be forgotten. The present trends and attitudes are apparently loaded heavily against narrowing.* (My italics—E.F.) The crises inherent in the economic gap are clearly not only persistent but even worsening. (42, p. 58)

Many other works treat the problem in much the same way, among them is *The Closed Circle* and a number of articles by

Commoner, and *Human Requirements, Supply Levels and Outer Bounds* by J. and M. McHale. In the introduction to the latter work, H. Cleveland writes:

> The growing debate about the content of a "new international economic order" still mostly consists of everybody talking at once, about his own problems, without relating them to the related problems of others. The facts of interdependence are bypassed in rhetoric about nation-states being "master in their own houses". Charges that the affluent consume too much provoke the countercharge that the poor have too many babies.
>
> But two themes are emerging which lend a special urgency to getting beyond debate to practical political accommodation. One is a hope—that the world community must somehow provide at least the minimum needs for every human being; "how much is enough" will be a prime subject for international negotiation. The other is fear—that under present assumptions and arrangements, world requirements for resources (including those to meet the "minimum needs") will transgress the "outer limits" of the natural environment to the detriment of future generations. (40, p. IV)

In "What Now?", a report on "another course of development", drafted by the Dag Hammarskjöld Foundation (50), the problem of bringing the economic and technical levels in the advanced and developing countries closer together is treated as most important and most urgent, although the authors of the report also speak about the difficulties arising in connection with the limited character of natural resources and the limited capacity of the environment.

Similar questions are raised in the *State of the Planet Statement* (draft) by Alexander King, Chairman of the Board of Trustees of the International Federation of Institutes of Advanced Study. This is what he writes:

> No, it is not growth as such, which is responsible for the present perils of society, nor is it technology which still remains the most powerful agent of mankind in its fight for

universal provision of its basic needs. Rather it is man's lack of wisdom in directing and managing growth and technology. The need is not to abolish growth—it is greatly needed in many parts of the world, but to check its excesses, to gear it to the quality of life and real global human needs and to bring it into equilibrium with possibilities and constraints. (37, p. 11)

All these problems are given detailed treatment in the paper "Reshaping the International Order", written by a group of scholars under Prof. J. Tinbergen at the request of the Club of Rome, and in a large number of articles.

Why is it that so many scholars and prominent public figures in advanced prosperous countries are concerned about the widening gap in living standards between the developed and the developing countries?

There are good reasons for this. Moved by humanitarian considerations, some authors cannot accept with equanimity the fact that hundreds of millions of human beings go hungry, live in ignorance, and are deprived of the most elementary benefits in a world which has enough resources to ensure a decent standard of living for all people, without exception.

And the others—who are, it seems, in the majority—feel alarmed in view of the impending danger to themselves as the result of serious crises that they fear might erupt in the near future. Mesarovic and Pestel write:

A more equitable long-term allocation of world resources would require that the industrialized regions put a stop to further overdevelopment by accepting limits on per capita use of finite resources. If development aid is to lend a truly helping hand to the hungry billions who must find a way out of their poverty, more than investment capital is needed. *Unless this lesson is learned in time, there will be a thousand desperadoes terrorizing those who are now rich, and eventually nuclear blackmail and terror will paralyze further orderly development.* (My italics—E.F.) Now is the time to draw up a master plan for organic sustainable growth and world development based on global allocation of all finite resources and a new global economic system.

Ten or twenty years from today it will probably be too late, and then even a hundred Kissingers, constantly crisscrossing the globe on peace missions, could not prevent the world from falling into the abyss of a nuclear holocaust. (42, p. 69)

The authors of "What Now?" take an interesting view of the events which led to a radical reassessment of the present situation in the world. The first such event, they say, is

the decision of OPEC to multiply the price of oil, if seen in the proper perspective. Its importance lies—more than in the price increases—in its character as a historic reversal.

In October 1973, the oil-exporting countries put an end to an era which had begun with what the West calls the 'great discoveries'. For the first time since Vasco da Gama, mastery over a fundamental decision in a crucial area of the economic policy of the center countries escaped their grasp as certain peripheral countries wrested it from them.

The second such development was

the outcome of the events in Indochina, where the peasants, spurred on by their will for independence, organised and freed themselves from the most formidable military and technological power that the world has ever known. (50, pp. 5-6)

Of course, we can hardly agree either with the authors' attempt to lump together the victory of the peoples of Indochina and OPEC's decision to raise the price of oil, or with their assertion that these events served as a turning point in the relations between the advanced countries and the developing countries which had been dependent on them either as colonies or, later, as economic appendages. Other, still earlier, events triggered this turn. But we shall return to this question later.

Further on in "What Now?" the authors speak about what in

their opinion caused this uneven economic development. They blame it on the present-day situation in our modern world:

> The existing "order" is coming apart, and rightly so, since it has failed to meet the needs of the vast majority of peoples and reserved its benefits for a privileged minority. The task is to create another one. (50, p. 6)

Commoner realizes that the impending environmental crisis is basically of socio-economic origin and is clearly tied up with other important economic and political problems of our time. He repeats again and again that private enterprise is unable to meet ecological needs, and writes:

> In effect, then, we now know that modern technology which is *privately* owned cannot long survive if it destroys the *social* good on which it depends—the ecosphere. Hence an economic system which is fundamentally based on private transactions rather than social ones is no longer appropriate and increasingly ineffective in managing this vital social good. The system is therefore in need of change. (26, p. 287)

Another article which attracted our attention is one written by physicist Edward Teller under the title "The Energy Disease". In it he looks att he causes of the present energy crisis as largely of socio-economic nature, and concludes his analysis of the situation with words bordering on the absurd:

> It is entirely possible that our system and our policies are inherently impractical.
>
> The predictions of the Communists may yet turn to be right. The free world may succumb to its own contradictions. In the event that we do not succumb, I am sure that the Communists are willing to do what they can to assist the process of collapse. They have encouraged OPEC (to raise the price of oil—*E.F.*), and they have every reason to do so. Not only are they apt to gain in their fight against capitalism, but they also are apt to profit by their oil exports (acting in this particular instance as monopolistic capitalists).

In the free-enterprise system, money means power, which is limited only by conventional rules. At the moment these conventional rules are producing changes which may ruin a number of advanced democracies. Millions may starve to death in the less developed countries. The free economic system may be challenged in a more terrible way than it was in the Great Depression. Then the Communists may get their first chance to take over the world: compared to the alternative of chaos, the cruel simplicity of Communism may gain almost universal appeal. (49, p. 17)

Edward Teller goes on to make a number of suggestions about drastic measures which must be taken in order to prevent what he considers such a terrible thing happening. Later in this account we shall discuss these measures in detail.

We have cited these excerpts from books and articles as samples of different views held by Western scientists. In all of these and many other works they assert that the serious global problems facing mankind today are interconnected in one way or another, and therefore must be resolved jointly by taking vigorous worldwide action.

The deeper they go into the problem the more these authors connect natural factors, technical progress, the depletion of natural resources, industrial impact on the environment, and questions of economic development with the economic, political and social conditions in the world.

In most of the Western studies and, as the reader can see, in all the sources quoted in this book, their authors, being non-Marxists, agree that today the free enterprise system (or the system of market relations, as many of them are inclined to call the capitalist system) is unable to cope with these problems.

Probably the clearest statement of all on this matter came from Dr. Aurelio Peccei, an Italian industrialist who is on the board of directors of several Italian firms, and who is even better known as the founder of the Club of Rome and its President. In one of his reports to the Club he said:

I do not think that the present neocapitalist structure and philosophy are capable of responding to the needs of our time. And, although I am not in a position to express a final judgement, I do not think that the structures as now exist in the socialist countries have that capacity either. (45, p. 52)

All the works quoted above say, in one form or another, that the optimal patterns of interaction with nature and high rates of development in the underdeveloped countries call for drastic changes in the social structure of society. It is worthy of note that the authors of these books express the view, though sometimes cloaked in verbal camouflage, that the development of human society is determined by certain objective laws governing this development.

For example, J. Forrester recommends rejecting the various intuitive ideas of the behavior of social systems and looking for objective laws of social development. Referring to the need to understand these laws he said: "Unless we understand and act soon, we may be overwhelmed by a social and economic system we have created but cannot control." (30, p. 8)

In the long preface to the paper, Reshaping the International Order written by a team of researchers under Prof. Tinbergen, they set forth their views on the laws governing social development. (51) However, neither Forrester nor the members of the Tinbergen team, nor any other authors of the books we have discussed seem to be serious about this problem.

In other words, when describing the process of social development and trying to find its tendencies, they somehow ignore the causes and mechanisms behind this process.

Aware that society develops in accordance with objective laws, although they themselves do not study these laws, the authors think it neither necessary to use them nor to criticize them. In fact they do not even mention the theory of social development which has been in existence for more than a hundred years, and which is being developed all the time and, what is most important, has been borne out by history itself. We refer, of course, to the theory of historical materialism originated by Marx and Engels and developed in the works of Lenin and in the works of outstanding theoreticians from many communist and workers' parties. Of course, we are far from expecting that all scholars will agree with this theory, and are therefore prepared to debate all aspects of this theory with its opponents. But to ignore the existence of a sufficiently well-known theory is, in our opinion, a rather quaint method of research on problems that obviously have a direct bearing on it.

Taking no account of the theory of historical materialism the above-mentioned authors, except for Commoner, shut their eyes to the practical achievements realized by the application of this theory. They are singularly uninterested in the activities of the socialist countries. In fact, they are not even curious to know what is being done there to create a balanced relationship between humans and nature. Nor do they see the difference in the character or in trends of development in countries with different social systems.

In their effort to give a general picture of the behavior of some sort of generalized global civilization, Forrester, Meadows and others apparently consider it redundant to particularize the distinctions between countries with different social systems. This would be acceptable if the laws governing social development and the progress of these social systems, at least where interaction with nature is concerned, were identical. This, however, is not so.

Mesarovic and Pestel take into consideration the variations in the initial stages of development in different countries, which they have grouped according to their degree of "affluence" (per capita national income, economic and technical progress). In this classification, the socialist countries of Europe comprise one such group.

The authors go on to discuss a number of situations which, according to them, might arise in all these groups of countries, given different rates of development (growth of the population, production and consumption). But here again they do not take into account the difference in the nature of the laws governing their development and rooted in the social systems of these countries. Having analyzed several "scenarios" of social and economic progress, they conclude that the leveling out of the development of what are at present backward countries and the industrially advanced nations by, say, reducing the rate of production and consumption growth in the latter, would in the long run prove the best way out for both groups.

The same pattern is followed in all the other works we have mentioned on prospects for the development of humanity.

All of them criticize the modern (universalized) attitude to the utilization of natural resources and to the environment, furnish facts of the dramatic differences between the economic, technical, living and cultural standards in the advanced ("rich", "industrialized", and "post-industrialized") countries and those in the developing("poor", "backward", etc.) countries. They also attempt to prove that in the present conditions the gap between these two main groups of countries may widen still further. And in addition to all that, the reader will be told about the great misfortunes for all humanity that this growing gap and disregard for ecological principles may eventually lead, and about what, in the opinion of the authors, must be done to even out differences in the living standards, including measures to fundamentally change, in some cases, the existing economic and social conditions.

We find it rather odd, however, that the authors, who, although they reckon with the fact that social and economic conditions also change in line with the objective laws of social development, at the same time ignore this important circumstance in their evaluation of the prospects for the future development of humanity.

Each of the above-mentioned works opens with the thesis that, unless the present *tendencies and character of the progress of mankind* are changed, the situation will be fraught with much trouble for the world, including a serious ecological crisis.

What shapes the character and the tendencies of growth and development of human society? And what do the authors assume will remain unchanged? Although the books in question do not contain a clear-cut definition of this immutable factor, we can well infer from the context that in the opinion of the authors this factor is the immutability of the existing social structure of society. To be more exact, this means that they assume the capitalist system as it exists in many countries today should continue in its present form, just as should the socialist system in the countries of the socialist community, and the various transitional forms of social organization in the developing countries.

The growth of population, production and consumption under these conditions will also widen the gap between the advanced and the developing countries and will precipitate an ecological catastrophe, they say.

In the light of the above, the question suggests itself: is the development of productive forces, including the growth of production and consumption, the growth of population and the development of technical progress, etc., possible for as long as several decades without changing the social structure? Historical materialism gives a negative answer to this question. And so does the entire history of humankind. Although in some individual countries the same social structure is known to have continued for a fairly long time, on the whole, social systems in the world are changing continuously at an accelerating pace.

To be able to understand the development of mankind in its perspective, we must choose a concept that would explain *the entire process of social development.*

For me, as well as for other Marxist researchers, this concept is the theory of historical materialism the correctness of which has been confirmed by the entire history of the past and present. The main factor in the development of society is the growth of productive forces (including labor resources, the means of production and the general level of scientific and technological progress). The growth of productive forces is responsible for the development of social systems. And the formation of a socio-economic system takes place within important social processes: the class struggle and the national liberation movement in capitalist society, the balanced planned development of the socialist system, and the competition between the two main social systems.

Therefore, it is impossible to evaluate perspectives of the development of society as a whole without due account being taken of all the other above phenomena. We would like here to emphasize again that interaction with the environment is a very important factor and phenomenon of progress, albeit not the only or main one. Concentrating as we do on the interaction of society with the natural environment, we try to assess the role of precisely this factor, and its possible influence on the development of humankind.

Now, what are the phenomena which have led to the present alarming situation in the interaction between man and nature, and to the dangerous gap in the living standards and economic development of different countries? Above, we discussed different views on this matter.

Forrester and Meadows consider that all social systems have one immanent quality: an urge to grow. Others say that this situation has been brought about by certain factors which disorganize social development, without so much as trying to establish the role of each one of these factors separately. Still others are of the opinion that this situation is the product of the very nature of humans and human society. And the last group of scholars blame the whole thing on the social system of capitalism.

It seems that all these views can well be summed up in this way: the main danger facing humanity and jeopardizing its development is the lack a mechanism to regulate the various activities of human society and its relationship with the natural environment. This leads to irrational utilization of the natural resources, to undesirable environmental changes, to widening the gap in living standards in different countries and to many other adversities.

We have become used to hearing about the unprecedented might of the human race today as the result of scientific and technological progress and the growth of productive forces. The forms of interaction with nature reviewed earlier in this account constitute only a few of many characteristics of humanity's might and ability to act, comparable in scope and impact to global natural processes and sometimes even more powerful.

Can we say when the immutable character of the development of mankind will lead to catastrophe? Hardly anyone will make bold to predict the time when all the constituent elements of the man-nature systems will come to a critical pass. However, we are much better equipped to discuss problems related to the ecological crisis.

As we pointed out before, people may come very near to using up the renewable natural resources (water, forest, soil and fish) in about 50 to 70 years. About this time the emission of industrial heat is expected to have a marked effect on the climate, which would be quite enough to create serious difficulties unless people learn how to control their activities.

Of course, this is a rather tentative estimate that we made

earlier on the basis of the same very simple considerations. Significantly, this estimate tallies with the time estimate of the extensive crisis which is described in one form or another in the books under review.

For our part, we can add that such a crisis may begin much earlier, in case of a serious military conflict, or may come later, if the climate actually begins to change. Thus, there is a very real danger that human society may transgress the admissible limits of its interaction with the environment in the not too distant future.

Neither Forrester nor the Meadows group are the first to have called attention to this circumstance. In their works written more than a hundred years ago, Marx and Engels for the first time formulated the thesis about the interconnection of social and natural factors in man's interaction with the environment, and raised the question of working out its optimal forms.

In a letter to Engels, March 25, 1868, Marx made this remark about the book of the Dutch agronomist Fraas:

> *Klima und Pflanzenwelt in der Zeit, eine Geschichte beide* (Climate and the Vegetable World Throughout the Ages, a History of Both), by Fraas (1847), is very interesting, that is as a demonstration that climate and flora have changed in *historic* times. He is a Darwinist before Darwin and makes even the *species* arise in historic times. But he is also an agronomist. He asserts that as a result of cultivation and in proportion to its degree, the 'moisture' so much beloved by the peasant is lost (hence plants migrate from south to north) and eventually the formation of steppes begins. The first effects of cultivation are useful, but in the end it lays the land waste owing to deforestation, etc. This man is both a very learned philologist (he has written books *in Greek*), and a chemist, agronomist, etc. The conclusion is that cultivation when it progresses spontaneously and is not *consciously controlled* (as a bourgeois he of course does not arrive at this), *leaves deserts behind it*—Persia, Mesopotamia, etc., Greece. (My italics—*E.F.*) Hence again socialist tendencies without being aware of them!...(2)

This quote can well apply to many present-day Western researchers of the problem of interaction between society and the natural environment. Just like Fraas they feel that the spontaneously developing culture leads to a crisis in the relationships between society and nature, and their calculations provide a fairly good illustration of just how this may happen. And, just like Fraas, they display (possibly unconsciously) certain "socialist tendencies".

They consider that the purely intuitive notions about the development of social systems should be discarded and that objective laws governing the behavior of these systems should, instead, be found. They think it necessary to revise the social values of the consumer society, to balance social processes, to use scientific and technological progress for the development of optimal forms of man's interaction with nature.

But Marx and Engels specifically pointed out that the progress of science and technology leads to a stage in the relationship between man and nature where society becomes quite able to draw practically the whole of the environment into the sphere of material production and in this way is able to exercise its influence on it. They pointed out that under capitalism this would result in a spontaneous, uncontrollable and therefore dangerous interference with nature, and that only with the establishment of common ownership of the means of production and of natural resources would society be able to create the most favorable conditions for a conscious and effective interaction between man and nature.

Marx wrote, in the third volume of *Das Kapital*:

> Freedom in this field can only consist in socialized man, the associated producers, rationally regulating their interchange with Nature, bringing it under their common control, instead of being ruled by it as by the blind forces of Nature; and achieving this with the least expenditure of energy and under conditions most favorable to, and worthy of, their human nature. (3)

Thus the authors of the materialist theory of social development regarded interaction (metabolism) between people and nature as a vital element of human life and activity and showed that the socialist organization of society would have every possibility to ensure optimal forms of such interaction.

Curiously enough, Meadows and others, in describing the more attractive features of "global equilibrium", said:

> The state of global equilibrium could be designed so that the basic material needs of each person on earth are satisfied and each person has an equal opportunity to realize his individual human potential. (41, p. 24)

They have forgotten altogether that Marx used much the same words in his brief characterization of a communist society of the future:

> In a higher phase of communist society, after the enslaving subordination of the individual to the division of labor, and therewith also the antithesis between mental and physical labor, has vanished; after labor has become not only a means of life but life's prime want; after the productive forces have also increased with the all-round development of the individual, and all the springs of cooperative wealth flow more abundantly—only then can the narrow horizon of bourgeois right be crossed in its entirety and society inscribe on its banners: 'From each according to his ability, to each according to his needs'. (4)

There is much more in the works of Marx and Engels than we have quoted here about interaction between man and nature.

And if the present order of things in the world cannot assure even a moderately comfortable existence for men on this earth and is to be replaced by another, then the question is how this replacement should be effected. Suggestions of this sort abound in the works we commented on and in many others recently put out in the West.

We shall concentrate on some aspects of these suggestions that, in our opinion, merit consideration.

We would like to begin with the idea advanced by Edward Teller who, as the reader may notice, stands out among many other authors.

Toward the end of his work on the present-day energy crisis,

Edward Teller calls upon the United States to pool all its available resources in order to meet its domestic energy needs, so as eventually to be able to start exporting fuel to other countries.

Further, he speaks about the need to set up a new order in the world.

> In trying to make a diagnosis of our serious condition I have said that the stability of the free economies in postwar years resulted from the benevolent leadership of one country, the United States. By 1985 the first great step toward curing the present energy disease may be completed, and the United States may have regained a similar measure of pre-eminence. But we cannot rest at that point.
>
> We have yielded our dominant position in the world once; if we regain it, we will have to yield it a second time. But this time we cannot risk chaos. *We must establish some form of world order*. The growth of technology has made a small neighborhood of our globe, and without some order there will be no peace in this neighborhood; the way of life as we like to imagine it will not survive. (My italics—*E.F.*) (49, p. 22)

As one may judge from this excerpt, and from the one quoted earlier, the author's concept is as simple as its formulation. The developing countries, prodded by the communists, raised the price of oil and caused economic trouble in the "free world". Development of such tendencies can lead to a collapse of the economy of the "free world", which will give the communists certain chances which might lead to their victory. The United States must, in the first place, pull out of the energy crisis and later, using all its capabilities, *regain its "pre-eminence" in the world and to establish a "world order" which will assure it a suitable "way of life"*.

Isn't this line of reasoning reminiscent of the philosophy which was so much in vogue in nazi Germany some forty years ago?

In our view the ideas of this world-famous physicist are just as naive as Goldsmith's (32) recommendation that people should go back to the primeval mode of living.

Prof. Teller may influence some people. However, the authors of the other works we commented on have different views on the problem. They too believe that a new world order should be established, but not for the purpose of preserving the American way of life in the United States. What they have in mind is an order which would serve the interests of the overwhelming majority of the population of our planet.

Thus, in their book John and Magda McHale write that a reconstitution of society must serve to promote the following "individual world rights" of every earth-dweller.

a) Each individual has the right "to a guaranteed decent share of the world's goods and services, irrespective of his occupation or contribution to society. This must ensure his food and shelter and opportunities for health, education, and cultural development."*

This statement recognizes that we are all heirs to the fruits of the human enterprise and its wealth, as this rests on the collective accumulated knowledge of all humankind. We are indebted today to the obscure Indian inventor of the zero in mathematics as we are to those who later invented the computer. This suggests that the human's birth certificate becomes his or her access credit card—to certain basic material and psychosocial needs.

b) There would follow upon this other rights. At a time when personal freedoms are in some danger of erosion, the consideration of human requirements must contain suitable provisions to protect the individual from political, economic, and other forms of coercion which abrogate his or her human rights. Most models of "world government" omit the necessity for somewhere to go if you happen to disagree with the world government! (40, p. 88)

The report "What Now?" singles out the following goals of "*another* development":

Development of every man and woman—of the whole man and woman—and not just the growth of things, which are merely means. Development geared to the satisfaction of needs beginning with the basic needs of the poor who

---

* Quoted by the McHales from the work published in the *Annals of the New York Academy of Sciences*, 184, June 7, 1971.

constitute the world's majority: at the same time, development to ensure the humanization of man by the satisfaction
of his needs for expression, creativity, conviviality, and for
deciding his own destiny. (50, p. 7)

In Commoner's view the discontinuation of the use of synthetic and other unnatural products and a transition to wider
use of natural materials will not only assure environmental
clean-up but will also raise the living standards in the developing countries, which are the main producers of natural raw
materials. The transformation of the economy, once started,
will stimulate the development of science, expedite the solution
of the necessary technical problems and will become, according
to Commoner, a self-sustained process. He goes on:

Moreover, we can expect that in an ecologically sound
economy, meaningful employment would become universally available. For once the principle is established—as
demanded by the ecological imperative—that production
is for social use rather than private profit or "plan fulfill-
ment", it would be clear that social good must begin with
the welfare of the people who make up society. (26, p. 288)

What can we say about these goals for the realization of
which the institution of a "new world order" is advocated? This
term, often used in the works of Tinbergen and other authors
must not be confused with the idea of "a new economic
order" brought forth by the developing countries. These are
good goals, the authors say, for they serve the interests of the
overwhelming majority of people in the world. Our planet has
enough natural resources and its environment has an adequate
"capacity" to meet these interests, as we attempted to prove in
the previous chapters. And this is what the authors of the books
referred to above accept for a fact.

To achieve these goals, the volume of both production and
consumption must grow in countries with low living standards.
This can be achieved only in the course of further scientific and
technological progress.

It is also necessary to organize long-range planning of all the
activities of humanity and to even out its development in differ-

ent areas. It is quite fair to assume that unless these goals are set and achieved the whole world may be threatened by a severe ecological crisis. In our view, Mesarovic and Pestel are quite right in saying that such crises are likely to begin on a local and regional scale.

To all intents and purposes, all the suggestions about the institution of a "new world order" are aimed at meeting the basic needs of the entire population of the earth by regulating the development of humankind and its activity so that it will not transgress the limits set by the existing resources of our planet. In the opinion of the authors, humanity should set itself a goal common for the whole of the population of the earth, and should take vigorous measures to achieve it.

And what could this be if not a call for a transition from the spontaneously developing to a consciously directed culture, which Karl Marx referred to a hundred years ago?

TOWARDS A CONSCIOUSLY DIRECTED CIVILIZATION

As we mentioned before, the authors we have been referring to ignored both the theory of historical materialism and the basic characteristics which mark the activities and development of socialist states and some developing countries, all of which together account for at least 50 percent of the world's population. Therefore, we shall have to recall what these authors wrote apropos of the problem under discussion.

Goal. No consciously directed development is possible without a goal to be achieved. And since capitalist social formation has no goal, the capitalist countries have no long-term comprehensive economic development program.

This has been discussed at length in the above-mentioned works. And such a leading Western politician and scholar as Henry Kissinger summed up the situation in these words:

> There is no doubt that the Western World is in deep trouble. It has not been able to articulate either a philosophy or a program adequate to our time. It has failed to identify itself with the revolutionary period through which we are living. It has not had the vision or the

willingness to carry through a sustained program to bring a sense of direction to a world in turmoil. (38)

Would it be correct to say that the main goal, or rather the main motivation for the development of the economy and the entire activities of the capitalist countries is that "urge to grow"? We don't think it would. Of course, the main incentive for the growth of production and consumption in capitalist society is a desire of the monopolies to extract greater profits, which fully accords with the interests of the military-industrial complex—that supermonopoly.

In contrast, socialist society has for a long time had a definite, clear-cut common goal, and a long-term program for its realization. In the USSR these goals are set forth in the Program of the Communist Party of the Soviet Union; they are specified and defined in the decisions of Party Congresses and later in five-year and annual economic development plans. Thus, prior to the 25th Congress of the CPSU, the targets for the development of the economy, culture and all the other principal aspects of the activities of Soviet society, especially with regard to the Tenth Five-Year Plan as formulated in the guidelines of the CPSU Central Committee, had been discussed by the whole Soviet nation for several months. Referring to that nationwide discussion of the guidelines for the development of the national economy of the USSR (1976-1980), before they were to be submitted to the Party Congress for consideration, the Chairman of the Council of Ministers of the USSR, Alexei Kosygin, said:

> This has been a truly nationwide discussion of the various aspects of our economic and social policy and the prospects and ways of development of our country's national economy. Our socialist society derives its strength from the consciousness of the masses, who in the words of Lenin "can form an opinion of everything and do everything consciously". (*Collected Works*, Vol. 26, p. 256) Lenin's idea was most forcefully borne out in the discussion of the draft "Guidelines" in which the working people expressed their views on an extensive range of questions of communist construction, displaying great

concern for the success of the common undertaking of the Party and the people, which is based on a profound understanding of the tasks before them. This is a vivid and convincing example of the effectiveness of socialist democracy, and one of its basic advantages over bourgeois democracy. Such a discussion is altogether inconceivable in any country of the capitalist world *even if only because of the limited class character of bourgeois democracy and the lack of political and socio-economic aims uniting the whole of society.* (My italics—*E.F.*) (8, p. 114)

Whatever views one may take of the goals which Soviet society has set itself, or the way we go about achieving them, the fact remains that these goals exist, they are known to everyone and, what is particularly important, these goals are accomplished. Sometimes they are accomplished more rapidly and more easily than expected, and sometimes more slowly and with greater effort. But accomplished they always are.

What are these goals? In describing the goals of the socialist system Lenin pointed out the need to organize a production process in a systematic planned manner in order to ensure high living standards and comprehensive and free development for all members of society.

A similar formulation is contained in the CPSU Program which is aimed at "satisfying the growing material and cultural reguirements of all members of society".

Doesn't this formula almost completely tally with what the above authors would like to put at the basis of a "new world order"? And what is still more important, the long-term plans for the country's development are truly aimed at the realization of these goals. For these are not merely the proposals of certain individual scientists or high-minded humanists, but goals approved by the whole people and by the ruling party, goals which underlie this nation's policy.

Long-term planning of the entire activities of a socialist state also accords with the "new world order".

Long-term planning promotes a steady rise in living standards and enables the socialist countries to meet to an ever greater degree the material and cultural needs of every member of socialist society.

As we mentioned before, socialist society, by its very nature, is interested equally in raising the effectiveness of production and the living standards of its members, and wherever necessary the production process is adjusted so as to keep it within ecologically safe limits.

It should be pointed out that, under socialism, planning is directed not only at *raising* the living standards, but also at *equalizing* the economic, technological and cultural levels both in different parts of a country and in different countries of the socialist community.

Following are some illustrations, based on the Russian Federation, the Kirghiz SSR and the Kazakh SSR, to give a broader picture of the development of the USSR. Before the revolution Kirghizia and Kazakhstan were the most backward regions of the Russian Empire, but in Soviet times the situation has changed dramatically. Between 1913 and 1973, per capita industrial output in the Russian Federation rose 113 times, in Kazakhstan 181 times and in Kirghizia 245 times. At the same time per capita gross output rose 3.2 times in Russia, 7.2 times in Kazakhstan and 6.5 times in Kirghizia. Between 1940 and 1973, the number of students per 10,000 of the population rose fivefold in Russia, ninefold in Kazakhstan and eightfold in Kirghizia. Between 1913 and 1973, the number of doctors per 10,000 of the population rose about 20 times (from 1.8 to 32.6) in Russia, 61 times (from 0.4 to 25.2) in Kazakhstan and 110 times (from 0.2 to 23.0) in Kirghizia. These and other facts show high rates of development not only in the USSR as a whole, but particularly high rates of development in the once backward regions.

The levels of development of these three republics of the Soviet Union were almost even in 1940, about 20 years after the establishment of Soviet power, and now there is practically no difference in the levels and rates of economic, technological and cultural development in these republics, as well as in all the other republics of the USSR.

Let's take a look at the rates of economic and technical development of the countries of the socialist community. Before

World War II, Romania and Bulgaria were the most backward of them all.

With per capita national income for 1950 taken as a basis, by 1973, it grew 6.3 times in the USSR, 7.4 times in Bulgaria and 8.1 times in Romania. During that period industrial per capita production in the USSR increased 8.5 times, in Bulgaria 15 times and in Romania 16 times. The output of the machine-building industry in these once predominantly agrarian countries increased 56 times in Bulgaria, 48 times in Romania and is much higher than the rate of increase in the USSR (18 times).

We could cite many more similar examples.

Thus Meadows' concept, and many other assertions to the effect that the growth of production and technical progress in general do not improve the lot of humanity, but rather widen the gap between the rich and the poor in every country and between countries, simply does not apply to the socialist community. The present character of the development of the social-its system not only promotes the general welfare, but also tends to bring the level of the most backward countries up to that of the most advanced, through accelerated growth of the economy in the less developed countries, and equalizing the living standards of different population groups in such countries.

And this does not happen spontaneously, but is the result of the consciously directed and regulated development of the economy and all other activities of socialist society. In the 1930s, for example, all the resources of our country were directed toward the development of heavy industry which manufactured producer goods. That was done not because our people had no need for clothes and other consumer goods. Not at all, these immediate needs were great and tended to drag our economy precisely in that direction. But a correct understanding of the long-term interests of society prompted our government to act as it did. And now Soviet people can reap the harvest of their effort and increase the production of consumer goods on the basis of the heavy industry they have built.

It is quite obvious that the conscious guidance, the optimal planning of the national economy of a country as large as ours is no simple matter. Efforts have been made to find new, more effective forms of economic management, and this, in turn, has created many problems and has even led to occasional mistakes. On the whole, however, the planning mechanism has worked successfully.

The other socialist countries are drawing on Soviet experience. It is also being utilized by the governments of many developing countries. Even government agencies in many capitalist states are studying our experience in order to make good use of it for their own purposes.

The proponents of the "new world order" or "new development" could also take into consideration that new forms of international relations between the socialist countries are taking shape.

This does not imply merely an offer of assistance in an emergency situation, but a constant, day-to-day exchange of information, know-how and commodities to make sure that the results of work done in one country will be of immediate benefit to all the others. There is no such thing here as a "brain drain" from the less developed into the more developed countries, a phenomenon which is contrary to common sense.

There is a large and steady flow of specialists from one socialist country to another: from more advanced enterprises and organizations to less developed ones. This assistance comes in different forms: from on-the-spot instruction over a certain period of time to studies at leading educational institutions. And if, some 20 to 30 years ago the Soviet Union was the only center the other socialist countries could turn to for know-how and assistance, now, with development at a more or less uniformly high level, this system has become polycentric. Division of labor and highly diverse mutual assistance between the socialist countries are becoming increasingly important elements of the international socialist system, whose economic relations are directed and stimulated by the Council for Mutual Economic Assistance.

It is wrong to judge the development of global systems and to design their future models from only the experience of one subsystem—the capitalist one—whose contribution to the world economy, percentagewise, is shrinking all the time.

It would be just as wrong, in our view, to divide all countries into "rich" and "poor" according to their national incomes, for this approach does not take into account the main distinctions in their socio-economic systems and the consequent specifics of their development.

It is also wrong to classify all the developing countries as "poor" and divide them into subgroups depending on the per capita national product. Of course, they have some common features, such as a low, and at times an extremely low economic, technical and cultural level. Hence their desire to overcome this backwardness, eliminate poverty and famine at all costs as soon as possible, and to provide the basic needs of their population. At the same time, each of these countries follows its own way of resolving this problem. Some of them, like most of the Latin American countries, have long since won nominal political independence, but have retained the capitalist social system which keeps them in economic bondage to the advanced nations, and especially to US monopolies.

At the same time, many countries in Africa and Asia which recently shook off the colonial yoke have set themselves the ultimate goal of building socialism and are now in various intermediate stages along their way to achieving this purpose. Precapitalist, capitalist and socialist socio-economic elements are peculiarly interwoven here into a complex, if fluid, social pattern. The possibilities for the development of the third-world countries, both in character and in degree, largely depend on how well a given social system is established there.

The cardinal objectives which require that present world economic and social conditions be changed were set by socialist society long ago. Many of these objectives have already been achieved; others are being achieved in the course of its development—both in the socialist countries individually and in the socialist community as a whole.

This similarity, if not identity, of goals could not go unnoticed by students of the modern socio-political structure of the world. Is it possible that they do not agree that these goals are similar? In that case it would be quite logical to expect them to study and analyze the elements that make them so different. However, we find nothing at all to this effect in any of the books we have been referring to. As we see it, this is explained not by any absence of information or incompetence, but rather by their reluctance to admit the simple fact that socialist society, and the socialist part of the modern world, has already accomplished or is on its way to accomplishing the principal tasks for the sake of which these authors have proposed a reorganization of the "world order". Also by their reluctance to admit that, should the whole world become socialist, the most difficult social aspects of the development problem, including the problem of optimizing relationships with nature, would be resolved, leaving mankind only the purely scientific and technical aspects to cope with.

All this goes to show that the authors of the proposals about a "new world order", "new development" and similar proposals are seeking a solution to the global problems of modern civilization only within the limits of the capitalist social system. The goals of a "new order" and "new development" and other proposed changes in the present-day economic and social system of the world are formulated in great detail, and their necessity is motivated from different points of view. The same cannot be said about the measures for their realization as formulated most exhaustively in the Tinbergen's paper and in all the other works we have referred to.

This is easy to understand, since the realization of the proposed goals indeed calls for serious and profound changes in the present-day international economic and political relations, and it would be naive to expect that concrete and universally acceptable recipes could soon be developed. With this important circumstance taken into account, we still think it necessary to make some critical remarks about them at this stage, too.

Let's take what seems to be a very simple question: setting a goal for humanity as a whole. As we mentioned earlier, the goals proposed by the authors of the works in question are on the whole both humane and rational. But we must add that not every society can set a certain goal for itself and achieve it, too. Setting a goal for the population of a country presupposes the community of interests and views of the whole of that population. Now, is this possible in a capitalist state? Striving for a "global" goal presupposes the full agreement of interests and views of humanity as a whole, for otherwise no goal can even be set. As for the achievement of such a goal, this calls for a worldwide effort to be made under one master plan, and also for a complex and painstaking reconstruction of the entire framework of society.

Having thus formulated the goal, society must then have a long-term perspective for its development. It is only then that it can assess the situation as a whole, or in a given sphere (e.g. the condition of the natural environment), favorable or unfavorable, both in our time and in the foreseeable future. Moreover, society must be able to plan and regulate the long-term development of its industry, agriculture, etc. on the whole of our planet, in accordance with the goal it has set itself.

Only then will it be able to utilize and multiply thriftily and effectively all of its resources, and particularly its natural resources, with due account being taken of world totals. Society must be in a position to utilize, when necessary, large amounts of material resources for the purpose of implementing joint projects in various parts of the planet—e.g., to effect expedient changes in the natural environment. And, finally, society must be free from major conflicts, since any of these will inevitably upset all the other conditions.

What social organization can meet all these conditions? In our opinion a worldwide socialist society would be the answer.

Now to some specific tasks.

To accelerate the development of the less developed countries, the authors suggest that the amount of aid be increased and its very character be altered. Most of them think it necessary to develop the industry, cultural facilities and educational system in these countries. They think, and quite justly so, that only in this way, and not by dispatching consumer goods there, can the advanced industrial nations help the developing countries get on their feet. This is precisely what the Soviet Union and the other socialist countries have been doing, to the best of their ability. Incidentally, the socialist countries have never exploited the natural wealth or the labor force of the developing countries, as did their former metropolitan masters.

The well-wishing authors tend to forget that what they call "development" is one of the aspects or, more precisely, the final stage of the national liberation movement, which is one of the most important elements of the social progress of humanity. Upon winning their independence, the developing countries have been consolidating their economic independence, and this includes their inalienable right to use their natural wealth for the good of their people.

Leonid Brezhnev noted in his Report to the 25th Congress of the CPSU that

> glancing at the picture of the modern world one cannot help noticing the important fact that the influence of states that had only recently been colonies or semi-colonies has grown considerably.
>
> It may definitely be said about the majority of them that they are defending their political and economic rights in a struggle against imperialism with mounting energy, *striving to consolidate their independence and to raise the social, economic and cultural level of their peoples.* (My italics—*E.F.)* (8, p. 216)

Are the industrial monopolies of the advanced capitalist countries genuinely interested in facilitating this process, i.e., to help build the industry of the developing countries and not their own? Didn't the national and multinational monopolies put up stiff resistance when the governments of developing countries nationalized the factories, agricultural estates and natural resources controlled by these monopolies? And did not this resistance by the foreign monopolies, more than any other thing, lead to the downfall of the governments of President Arbenz in Guatemala and the Allende goverment in Chile?

Where the developing countries clearly need assistance most of all is in eliminating outdated social and economic patterns, such as big landownership, usury, tribalism, etc.

But what is even more important is that the newly independent countries not be obstructed in their efforts, using progressive methods, to build up their economies. This means that the foreign monopolies must relinquish their control of natural resources which rightfully belong to the people of the developing countries. Finally, the despoiled countries must receive some recompense from the industrially advanced nations and the monopolies for the colossal profits reaped by exploiting their natural wealth and manpower during decades or even hundreds of years of colonial rule.

The suggestions made by some of the authors, that the "rich" countries should limit consumption and hand over the resources thus saved to the "poor" countries, sound very noble indeed.

The report "What Now?", for example, suggests that Sweden set an example by abolishing the right to own private cars and by reducing the consumption of meat through the institution of special "meatless days".

The point is, whose consumption should be limited? Could it not happen, for instance, that millions of unemployed and poor people in the "rich" countries would demand that these resources should first be used to improve their lot?

Most of the "rich" capitalist countries, like the United States, cannot, or rather do not even consider it necessary, to seek out resources to supply the elementary needs of their own poor whose number, incidentally, is not that small or to provide all their citizens with free medical care and education, which, by the way, has long since been done in all the socialist countries.

It should be borne in mind that a reduction in the volume of consumption cannot be effected without the consent not only of the people of the advanced countries but also of the capitalist monopolies which manufacture consumer goods, for such a reduction would inevitably cause profits to go down. Now, is it possible to secure such consent?

The Tinbergen team has made a number of suggestions (in its Report R10-19, for example) on the just, equitable satisfaction of the needs of the earth's population for good. These suggestions include the creation of world food stocks, world reserves of fertilizers, a reduction in the consumption of meat in the advanced countries, etc. Tinbergen also tries to prove that, if all these suggestions were translated into life, the needs of the entire population of the earth would be satisfied. This, of course, is all true. But it is also true that for it to happen the capitalist monopolies and the governments of the advanced Western countries would have to voluntarily relinquish their own selfish interests for the benefit of all.

But how would decision-makers in the United States and other advanced capitalist countries look at this?

The French weekly *Le Point,* on February 9, 1976, carried an article under the headline: "Wheat: the Ultimate Weapon", which analyzed statements made by Earl L. Butz, US Secretary of Agriculture.

After a long tour of the countries of Europe and the Middle East, in December 1975, Earl Butz said that the rate of consumption there was growing rapidly and the demand for quality food items was growing, too. These are good buyers of American wheat and of meat from cattle raised on American soy beans. Earl Butz went on to say that all the American food which the United States was handing out to these countries in the form of aid should be used for the purpose of drawing them into the sphere of American influence. According to Mr. Butz, that would be a good investment.

There is no doubt that such ideas have already been put into practice. In his book *By Bread Alone,* Lester Brown points out that in 1973 the United States turned down the request of Chile's President Allende for a supply of wheat on credit. Lester Brown continues:

> Since Chile's foreign-exchange reserves were then exhausted and bread shortages were developing, this American action undoubtedly contributed to the downfall of the Allende government in September, 1973. Although Americans decry the use of petroleum as a political weapon, calling it 'political blackmail', the United States has been using food aid for political purposes for twenty years—and describing this as 'enlightened' diplomacy. (23)

It is well known today that the delay in the shipment of wheat was one of many economic actions taken by multinational monopolies and the reactionary quarters in the United States in order to overthrow the lawful progressive government of Chile. There are many more examples of this sort.

The authors of a "new world order" and "new development" attach a great deal of importance to the functions of international organizations. The conclusion they have arrived at is twofold. In the first place, international organizations, beginning with the United States and its specialized agencies, must be vested with greater authority. The authors propose that new agencies be set up to promote utilization of natural resources in the interests of humanity and that eventually an international organization with worldwide powers be created to put this exploitation of resources on a planned footing. Second, the sovereign rights of countries, especially in matters of exploitation of resources and economic development, must be curtailed.

The authors' main mistake is, we think, in their proposing some sort of global "regulation" of humanity's activities, which in fact is opposed to the sovereignty of individual countries. And although they often refer to "voluntary" concessions of some sovereign rights by nations to international bodies, they in effect propose the creation of a supranational mechanism with authority to impose its own mandatory solution to problems with regard to the economic activities of states and to the utilization of their natural resources.

In our view, it would be proper to speak about cooperation between nations rather than about "international regulation" imposed from above, which infringes on the sovereign rights of nations. Countries can coordinate their actions on a global scale only if their relations are based on equal and mutually advantageous cooperation. It has been proved in practice that when peoples and their governments are aware of the need for and the advantages of certain joint actions, they do their utmost to make such actions possible. The Universal Postal Union, the International Telecommunications Union, the World Health Organization, the World Meteorological Organization and many others work successfully, coordinating and unifying the activities of countries in their respective fields.

It is more difficult to coordinate international relations in areas that affect the political and economic interests of countries, and still more difficult when interests of national security are involved. Of course, the reason for this does not lie in the absence of relevant international organizations.

The structure of the United Nations is basically suitable for considering and adopting decisions in this sphere. It has adopted many rational decisions, such as those in support of the decolonization process and in support of the rights of the Arabs exposed to Israeli aggression, and many others.

Regrettably, even these decisions are often not carried out after they are adopted. They are sabotaged by those who consider these decisions unsuitable for reasons of profit, by those who rely on the assistance and patronage of big powers. Such are the attitudes of the South African government and the regime of Ian Smith, which was long entrenched in Rhodesia, and also of the Israeli government.

It is not the UN structure that is bad, but the fact that certain major states have not yet relinquished their positions-of-strength policy, in the hope that such a stand will serve their interests at the expense of other countries and peoples.

The authors of the books we have referred to are at pains to work out a long-term program or project for the development of humanity. Their line of argument in support of this program calls to mind Lenin's words:

> ...there were many dreamers, some of them geniuses, who thought that it was only necessary to convince the rulers and the governing classes of the injustice of the contemporary social order, and it would then be easy to establish peace and general well-being on earth. They dreamt of a socialism without struggle. (7)

Does this mean that the idea of coordination of human activities on a global scale is unrealistic? No, it does not.

Using all the key factors of the development of human society, the doctrine of historical materialism has proved that at a certain stage of its development the entire population of the earth must be and inevitably will be integrated into one single socialist system.

Does this mean that we propose to establish a worldwide socialist system now, without delay, in response to the proposals under discussion? Not at all. The teachings of historical materialism and indeed the history of human society clearly show that socialism cannot be established by decree or by force. Socialism will emerge only when the majority of the people have become convinced on the basis of a number of factors that this new social system is the only acceptable one, and when they are prepared to work and fight for this conviction with every means at their disposal.

The socialist system eliminates the problems in question. This, however, does not mean that we should wait for socialism to become a worldwide system, for a great deal of work can be done already now. Many Western scientists, political writers and public leaders share the opinion that humanity should be integrated under a single social system based on scientific principles.

This is what Prof. Commoner, whom we have mentioned many times, said:

> The lesson of the environmental crisis is, then, clear. If we are to survive, ecological considerations must guide economic and political ones. And if we are to take the course of ecological wisdom, we must accept at last the even greater wisdom of placing our faith *not in arms that threaten world catastrophe, but in the desire that is shared everywhere in the world—for harmony with the environment and for peace among the peoples who live in it.* (My italics—*E.F.*) Like the ecosphere itself, the peoples of the world are linked through their separate but interconnected needs to a common fate. The world will survive the environmental crisis as a whole, or not at all. (26, p. 292)

This excerpt contains a rather important and at the same time very simple thought: the greatest wisdom is that of placing our faith not in the arms that threaten world catastrophe but in the desire for peace among the peoples.

The same idea is voiced, in one form or another, in most of the other works we have mentioned in this book. However, neither Commoner nor any of the other authors devote sufficient attention to it. The impression is that they regard peace as an element of some sort of universal bliss which will be consequent upon the attainment of the proposed "new world order", "new development" and other such projects. Thus, the whole situation is put upside down. Do they really think it possible to achieve full agreement of views on serious economic and political problems that concern different countries, to set one common goal for all humanity and to achieve it worldwide amid crippling international tension, the danger of war and the arms drive?

Is it not clear that the elimination of these factors and the creation of conditions which rule out the very possibility of a global thermo-nuclear conflict; halt, or at least considerably reduce the arms drive; make detente irreversible, and ensure not only peaceful coexistence but also close cooperation between countries with different social systems—would enable these countries to set common goals for all mankind and to take concerted joint actions for their realization.

Is it not clear that by curbing the arms race and reducing military budgets, which absorb hundreds of billions of dollars every year, we would be able to save quite substantial and sufficient means to assure such actions for common goals?

The world needs great changes, and these are taking place all the time. The process of social development of humanity continues unabated. But this process can be impeded by helping the reactionary forces which try to hold back social development. One such example was the war against the peoples of Vietnam. Another is Israel's attempts to reverse the social and economic development of the Arab countries. On the other hand, this process can be facilitated by helping the national liberation movement of the peoples in the developing countries, by promoting the development of their industry and training their national personnel, etc.

This process cannot be stopped or even delayed, and much less reversed. It is impossible to stop the revolutionary movement in countries where the people have become aware of its necessity and are prepared to defend it with all the means at their disposal—from parliamentary elections to an armed struggle. For this movement cannot be "organized" artificially with means brought from without.

Many readers may not agree with the Marxists, who believe in the inevitability of the social development of humanity when all countries will be part of a worldwide socialist system. As a matter of fact, we are not trying to convince them of that.

However, in our day and age, social progress obviously has reached a stage when a lasting peace between nations, disarmament, coexistence, and close cooperation between states with different social systems are quite possible.

This has come about as a result of the development of many processes, all of which taken together constitute what we call the social progress of mankind. The economic and technical strength of the Soviet Union and the other socialist countries has rendered ineffective the "positions-of-strength" policy which some forces would like to carry on even now. (This is why Professor Teller's ideas, mentioned earlier, sound rather naive.) The victories scored and still being scored by the peoples of former colonies in the national-liberation struggle and in the not less arduous struggle for economic independence against superior adversaries necessitate a transition from the policy of *diktat* to cooperation.

The successes being scored in the class struggle of working people in capitalist countries for the improvement of their material conditions, against unemployment, and against the power of the monopolies, strengthen and develop all the elements of democracy in the social systems of these countries.

We would like to single out here the role played by the growing efficacy and influence of world public opinion.

Most of the people of my generation, those who lived through and fought in World War II, were convinced that it would be the last war in the history of man. Therefore there was a prompt and powerful response by the progressive public everywhere to the efforts of the reactionary forces in the United States and Great Britain to unleash a cold war and other cold and "hot" conflicts.

It was at that time that the mass movement for peace—at the source of which stood such outstanding scientists, humanists and public leaders as Frédérick Joliot-Curie, Yves Farge, Ilya Ehrenburg and many others—was born. But though it assumed vast proportions in Europe and in many developing countries, this movement, for a number of reasons, did not develop in the United States. However, the United States saw the rise of another movement, the Pugwash movement of leading scientists in all countries against war and for cooperation between nations. The Pugwash movement originated on the initiative of the financier and industrialist Cyrus Eaton. Also, at that time many hundreds of national and international societies, unions and movements came into being to defend the cause of peace, each from its own moral, religious, humanitarian or ideological positions. Many of these organizations and movements exist to this day.

Lately they have more and more often joined efforts in support of peace and the national liberation struggle of oppressed peoples, and in defense of human rights. One such demonstration of unity was the World Congress of Peace Forces held in Moscow in 1973.

All these and many other elements of social progress have created a situation in which the elimination of the threat of war, an abatement of the arms drive, and further consolidation of cooperation between the peoples have become quite realistic, and attainable in the foreseeable future.

The principles of peaceful coexistence of states with different social systems are becoming the norm in international relations.

The Helsinki conference on security and cooperation in Europe affirmed the principles of cooperation between states. These principles have provided ample opportunities for joint discussion and solution of the serious problems facing all nations of the world.

By signing the European Charter for Peace (Final Act), the heads of thirty-three European nations, and also the USA and Canada, assumed commitments in a wide spectrum of questions, some of them relating to the protection of nature and rational utilization of its resources.

The Soviet Union and the United States have long since been negotiating a reduction in the growth of strategic weapons. This is a difficult problem, but the two most powerful nations of the world have shown goodwill for its solution, which gives us hope that this problem ultimately will be resolved. Talks are also being conducted with a view to reducing armaments and armed forces in Europe.

An international agreement has been signed banning the use of chemical weapons, and more agreements are being considered on banning the development of new types and systems of weapons. A good deal of work has been done and more still is being done to resolve some specific problems involved in limiting the arms race, and to further reduce the threat of thermonuclear war.

Of course, more progress could have been made. But we hope that a world disarmament conference will help resolve this vital issue. We firmly believe that the solution of the key problems of peace, disarmament and cooperation between countries with different social systems should serve as the basis for implementing any worldwide projects or any global actions including those which may optimize the relations between man and nature or to equalize the living standards in different countries, which has been indicated many times in the works on which we commented.

This thesis was clearly formulated by Leonid Brezhnev in a speech at the World Congress of Peace Forces. He said:

> But peace is not only a question of security. It is also the most important prerequisite for solving the most crucial problems of modern civilization. And here the very future of humanity is involved.... Here it will be sufficient to mention but a few of the problems that are beginning to cause many people concern: energy supply, environmental protection, elimination of such blights as mass hunger and dangerous diseases, and development of the resources of the World Ocean. (10)

There is no other way out. And here is what Leonid Brezhnev said at the 25th Congress of the CPSU:

> Assessing our country's international situation and world conditions, the Party's Central Committee considers that *further struggle for peace and the freedom and independence of the peoples now requires first of all fulfilment of the following vital tasks:*
>
> — While steadily strengthening their unity and expanding their all-round cooperation in building the new society, the fraternal socialist states must augment their joint active contribution to the consolidation of peace.
>
> — Work for the termination of the expanding arms race, which is endangering peace, and for transition to reducing the accumulated stockpiles of arms, to disarmament. For this purpose:
>
> a) do everything to complete the preparation of a new Soviet-US agreement on limiting and reducing strategic armaments, and conclude international treaties on universal and complete termination of nuclear weapons tests, on banning and destroying chemical weapons, on banning development of new types and systems of mass annihilation weapons, and also banning modification of the natural environment for military or other hostile purposes;
>
> b) launch new efforts to activate negotiations on the reduction of armed forces and armaments in Central

Europe. Following agreement on the first concrete steps in this direction, continue to promote military detente in the region in subsequent years;

c) work for a switch from the present continuous growth of the military expenditure of many states to the practice of their systematic reduction;

d) take all measures to assure the earliest possible convocation of a World Disarmament Conference.

— Concentrate the efforts of peace-loving states on eliminating the remaining seats of war, first and foremost on implementing a just and durable settlement in the Middle East. In connection with such a settlement the states concerned should examine the question of helping to end the arms race in the Middle East.

— Do everything to deepen international detente, to embody it in concrete forms of mutually beneficial cooperation between states. Work vigorously for the full implementation of the Final Act of the European Conference and for greater peaceful cooperation in Europe. In accordance with the principles of peaceful coexistence continue consistently to develop relations of long-term mutually beneficial cooperation in various fields—political, economic, scientific and cultural—with the United States of America, France, the FRG, Britain, Italy, Canada, and also Japan and other capitalist countries.

— Work for ensuring Asian security based on joint efforts by the states of that continent.

— Work for a world treaty on the non-use of force in international relations.

— Consider as crucial the international task of completely eliminating all vestiges of the system of colonial oppression, infringement of the equality and independence of peoples, and all seats of colonialism and racialism.

— Work for eliminating discrimination and all artificial barriers in international trade, and all manifestations of inequality, *diktat* and exploitation in international economic relations.

These, comrades, are the main tasks, the attainment of which, as we see it, is essential at present in the interests of peace and security of peoples, and the progress of mankind. We consider these proposals an organic projection and development of the Peace Program advanced by our 24th Congress, *a program of further struggle for peace and international cooperation and for the freedom and independence of the peoples.* We shall direct our foreign policy efforts towards achieving these tasks, and shall cooperate in this with other peace-loving states.

Permit me to express confidence that the lofty aims of our policy on the international scene will be received with understanding and win the wholehearted support of all the peace-loving, progressive forces, and all honest people on earth. (8, pp. 30-32)

This is not the opinion of an individual scientist, humanist or public leader, but a guideline for the basic, long-term goals of the foreign policy of the Soviet Union, a guideline which was discussed and unanimously approved by the 25th Congress of the CPSU. These ideas are an extension of the Program of Peace adopted at the 24th Congress, a program which won worldwide acclaim, and which has since been translated into life.

Our readers may well agree that the adoption and implementation of programs like this by other countries would greatly advance the cause of peace and cooperation between peoples.

Those are the possibilities which mankind has at the present stage of its social development. Their realization would help solve many problems of modern civilization, including the problems discussed in this book.

Therefore we consider that it is not the development of complex social and economic schemes, or the creation of supranational bodies, nor is it the advocacy of limited sovereignty or reorganization of the United Nations and its agencies, but the struggle for peace, for an end to the arms drive, for disarmament, and for making detente irreversible that must be the principal objective of those who are concerned about any aspect of the immediate future of humanity.

Speaking about the development of humanity over the long term, we concur with the views of many scholars and political writers who regard the emergence and development of life in

general and its highest form—human society—as a logical stage
in the development of the universe, and not merely as an accidental phenomenon or an "illness of senile matter".

In his remarkable work *The Poetry of Science,* the Soviet auth-
or H. F. Hilmi wrote:

> No matter what place chaosogeneity might hold in the
> universe, the emergence of life in its chaosogenic regions
> is not an accidental phenomenon, but the legitimate result
> of the development of matter.
>
> The simplest primary forms of the organization of mat-
> ter appeared back in the physical stage of development.
> Nuclear and molecular forces are the principal organizing
> factors in the microcosm, just as the forces of gravitation
> are in the macrocosm. And later, in the depths of the chaos-
> ogenic parts of the macrocosm there originate the simplest
> cybernetic systems which are capable of adapting them-
> selves to new conditions and balance out the effects of the
> environment. From these cybernetic systems, by means of se-
> lection and evolution, life arises and develops.
>
> The chaosogenic medium legitimately generates its dia-
> lectical negation: the living systems which overcome the
> chaosogeneity of the universe.... And is the idea all that
> crazy that the emergence of life in the chaosogenic regions
> of the universe means the birth of a new stage in its devel-
> opment? It is possible that life, especially its higher forms,
> is destined to organize the universe by activity expanding
> and consolidating the sphere of its propagation. This idea
> may sound preposterous now for the same reason that a
> prophecy to the effect that man would be able to organize
> the natural environment on a global scale would have sound-
> ed preposterous to our ancestors who lived a mere one or
> two thousand years ago. (18)

It would hardly be possible to find arguments that could prove
that such prospects for the development of mankind are ill-judged.
Over the next 100 years man will have to take yet another very
important step on this long road: to become the organizer of
nature on the whole of our planet. And this can be achieved, as

we have seen, only in the form of an organized society capable of regulating its own development and its interaction with nature, in the form of a consciously developing civilization.

Can society retain its capacity for multiple, even though regulated, development? Most of the students in our field of research, like this author, would give an affirmative reply to this question.

Perhaps, because the possibilities for converting different substances into sources of energy grow much faster than the depletion of certain types of raw materials and sources of energy (the reserves of which will continue to grow for a long time yet), while the expenditure of nonrenewable resources on our planet will long continue to be negligible, and can be compensated for by using the resources of outer space.

Perhaps because environmental pollution can be reduced to negligible levels, while the pollution-induced changes in the balance of matter and in the balance of energy can be suitably neutralized.

Or perhaps because cultivation of renewable natural resources and their proper balancing make it possible to raise many times over the productivity of nature as a whole.

In other words, a well-organized society which consciously directs its own progress will have enough capabilities for diversified development on earth and outer space as well.

In conclusion, I would like to go back to Academician Vernadsky and cite the remarkable thesis he formulated back in 1944.

> The historical process is changing right before our eyes. For the first time in history, the interests of the masses of men taken as a whole and individually, and the free thought of the individual determine the life of mankind and serve as a yardstick for its ideas of justice.
>
> Man is growing into a mighty geological force. He, his thought and labor, are confronted with the task of restructuring the biosphere for the benefit of an integrated, free-thinking mankind....
>
> The ideals of our democracy are in unison with the spontaneous geological process, with the laws of nature. Therefore we can look to the future with confidence. For the future is in our hands and we shall not let it go. (13)

BIBLIOGRAPHY

1. K. Marx and F. Engels, *Selected Correspondence*, Moscow, 1975, p. 315.
2. K. Marx and F. Engels, *Selected Correspondence*, Moscow, 1975, p. 190.
3. Karl Marx, *Capital*, Vol. III, Moscow, 1974, p. 820.
4. K. Marx and F. Engels, *Selected Works*, Vol. 3, Moscow, 1976, p. 19.
5. V. I. Lenin, *Collected Works*, Vol. 5, Moscow, p. 110.
6. V. I. Lenin, *Collected Works*, Vol. 27, Moscow, pp. 320-321.
7. V. I. Lenin, *Collected Works*, Vol. 2, Moscow, p. 20.
8. *Documents and Resolutions. The 25th Congress of the CPSU*, Novosti Press Agency Publishing House, Moscow, 1976.
9. L. I. Brezhnev, *Following Lenin's Course*, Moscow, 1972, p. 35.
10. L. I. Brezhnev, *Following Lenin's Course*, Moscow, 1975, pp. 325-326.
11. Будыко М. И., *Влияние человека на климат*, Л., Гидрометеоиздат, 1972.
12. Вернадский В. И., *Биохимические очерки*, М., Изд. АН СССР, 1944, стр. 38.
13. Вернадский В. И., *Несколько слов о ноосфере. Успехи современной биологии*, т. 18, в. 2, 1944.
14. Воейков А. И., *Воздействие человека на природу*, М., Географгиз, 1949, стр. 87.
15. «Новое время», № 1, 1951, стр. 22.
16. Урланис Ц., В сб. *Марксистско-ленинская теория народонаселения*, М., «Мысль», 1971.
17. Федоров Е. К., *Взаимодействие общества и природы*, Л., Гидрометеоиздат, 1972; Федоров Е. К., *Экологический кризис и социальный прогресс*, Л., Гидрометеоиздат, 1977.
18. Хильми Г. Ф., *Поэзия науки*, М., «Наука», 1971, стр. 49.
19. Хильми Г. Ф., «Философские проблемы преобразования природы», Сб. *Взаимодействие наук при изучении Земли*, Изд. АН СССР, М., 1963.
20. Циолковский К. Э., *На Луне*, М., стр. 40.
21. Baade F., *Der Wettlauf zum Jahre 2000*, 2 durchgesehene Auflage, Berlin, 1968.
22. Bekele M., "False Prophets of Doom", *The UNESCO Courier*, July-August, 1974.
23. Brown L., *By Bread Alone*, New York, Washington, Praeger Publishers, 1974, p. 69.
24. Calder R., "Mortgaging the Old Homestead", *Foreign Affairs*, Vol. 48, No. 2, January 1970, pp. 207-220.

25. Clarke A., *Profiles of the Future*, New York, Harper and Row Publishers, 1962, pp. 12-21.

26. Commoner B., *The Closing Circle*, New York, Alfred Knopf, 1971.

27. Dorst J., *Avant que nature meure*, Delachaux et Niestle, Neuchatel (Switzerland), 1970, pp. 33-34.

28. Fairchild H. P., *The Prodigal Century*, New York, Philosophical Library, 1950, p. 15.

29. Folk R., *Planet Under Peril*, New York, Random House, 1971.

30. Forrester J., *World Dynamics*, Wright Allen Press, 1971.

31. Goldman M., *The Spoils of Progress: Environmental Pollution in the Soviet Union*, The MIT Press, 1972.

32. Goldsmith E., *The Crisis of the Industrial Society, Peace and the Sciences, Global Problem of Modern Civilisation*, Lnternational Institute for Peace, Vienna, 1974.

33. Hardin G., "The Immorality of Being Softhearted", *The Relevant Scientist*, Vol. 1, November 1971, p. 18.

34. Harrya J.-P., *Afrique. Terre qui Meurt*, Bruxelles, 1949.

35. Hugenheim, *Bulletin of the American Meteorological Society*, 1953.

36. Jeans J., *The Stars in Their Courses*, Cambridge, 1931.

37. King A., *State of the Planet Statement*, First Draft, JFIAS, 1975.

38. Kissinger H., *The Necessity for Choice. Prospects of American Foreign Policy*, New York, 1968, p. 98.

39. Linnemann H., "Food for a Doubling World Population", Preparatory paper for the Club of Rome, Free University of Amsterdam, May 14, 1975.

40. McHale J. and McHale, Magda Cordell, *Human Requirements, Supply Levels and Outer Bounds, A Policy Paper*, Aspen Institute for Humanistic Studies, 1975.

41. Meadows D. H., Meadows D. L., Rander J., Behrens W., *The Limits to Growth*, New York, Universe Book, 1972.

42. Mesarovic M., and Pestel E., "Mankind at the Turning Point", The second report to the Club of Rome, New York, Reader's Digest Press, 1974.

43. Odum, Eugene P., *Fundamentals of Ecology*, Third Edition, Philadelphia-London-Toronto, W. B. Saunders Company, pp. 46-47.

44. Oser J., *Must Men Starve? The Malthusian Controversy*, London, Jonathan Cap., 1956, p. 23.

45. Peccei A., *Some Basic Concepts Which May Be Useful in Approaching Contemporary Global Problems, Peace and the Sciences*, International Institute for Peace, Vienna, Symposium, Global Problems of Modern Civilisation, March 1974.

46. Revelle R., "Can the Earth Feed the Growing Multitudes?", *The UNESCO Courier*, July-August 1974, p. 9.

47. Ruhle O., *Brot für sechs Milliarden*, Urania-Verlag, Leipzig-Berlin, 1961, S. 112-113.

48. Saada P., *El Universal*, 25 apr. 1970.

49. Teller E., "The Energy Disease", *Harper's Magazine*, February 1975.

50. The 1975 Dag Hammarskjöld Report, "What Now?" Another Development. Development Dialogue. *A Journal of International Development Cooperation,* Uppsala, 1975, No 1/2.

51. Tinbergen J.—coordinator, "Reshaping the International Order (RIO)". A report to the Club of Rome, No. 9, 1976.

52. Toynbee A., "The Religious Background of the Present Environmental Crisis", *International Journal of Environmental Studies,* 1972, Vol. 3, p. 141.

53. U Thant, "Report: Problems of the Human Environment, Economic and Social Council (ECOSOC)", Doc. E/4667, 26. 5. 1969, p. 8.

54. Vignes J., *L'Afrique et l'Asie,* January 10-13, 1972.

55. "Weather Modification". Hearings before the subcommittee on oceans and international environment of the Committee on Foreign Relations, United States Senate, January 25 and March 20, 1974, Washington, 1974.

56. "Weather Modification as a Weapon of War". Hearings before the subcommittee on inernational organizations and movements of the Committee on Foreign Affairs of Representatives, September 24, 1974, Washington, 1974.

57. Woytinsky W. S. and Woytinsky E. S., *World Population, Trends and Outlook,* 1955, p. 329.

Soc
GF
41
F42